A]

MW01233796

or

SURVIVING THE COMING NUCLEAR WAR

The hand guide to surviving the soon-to-come atomic war and the chaos to follow

TARL WARWICK
2015

DISCLAIMER

CONTENTS

INTRODUCTION

Those with a bit of common sense know that at this point, a world nuclear war or some other catastrophe is inevitable- it's the same old story over and over, if man doesn't manage to completely destroy or at least cripple himself, it's only a matter of time before some cosmic event wipes out large proportions of humanity. In the most amusing possible scenario, our technology is capable of allowing just a few nations to pound one another with multi-megaton warheads, causing widespread chaos and extermination, yet our technology leaves in doubt our ability to destroy, say, a world-ending asteroid; one which is surely out there somewhere, hurtling through space.

Because it's unlikely that anyone at all would survive such a cosmic event anyways it suffices here to note that other than a few astronauts, everyone else here would be in severe peril were a nuclear war to erupt. I will explain in this text why I feel this is not a possibility but an *inevitability* and attempt here to save as many lives as possible by making some suggestions for those who do manage to ride out the exchange, in the hopes that future generations will emerge, clean up the mess of the present, and build a world not quite as insane as the one we currently live in, where a handful of people can doom the rest of mankind despite having apparently limited mental faculties.

In the confused state of the modern world many mistakes have been made; elections have become corrupt, militaries more ferocious, projective capability is now unlimited, save for space- even space may end up weaponized in the future, unless nuclear war wipes man out before anyone is able to do so. We spend money propping up governments that, by and large, don't really represent our interests and represent instead a sort of loosely competitive conglomerate of industrial heads and political leaders, twain with, of course, religious leaders who help them achieve their ends.

Sadly even a world revolution- a revolution involving all people in all nations rising up en masse- would not solve the problem. Like a cancer, only a small sliver of the tumor of corruption has to remain for it to eventually emerge anew; such is the struggle of man, for it has ever been the same. In fact, only a complete wiping out of man, or an event very closely akin to it, would even disarm the world of its weapons- there's no guarantee that this would prevent rearmament perhaps centuries later. There's the rub; this work may be in vain because in the long expanse of time, even after such a war, another might occur and finish what the first did not. There are some who feel that if we encounter the ruins of alien civilizations somewhere in space that the odds of extra terrestrial life ever being long lasting is far lower; it may be that aliens surmise the same and will eventually find the radioactive, charred remnants of our culture and remark with sadness that their own doom follows.

This work may be seen as one part basic survival guide, one part philosophical manifesto, and one part political and social rumination- the bearer of ill news is often a quite unwelcome guest, but this does not mean the person bearing such news is wrong, or somehow in error- it is a simplistic notion, of specifically why nuclear war, should it not be precluded by other catastrophe first, is inevitable. As such, I produce this book.

For my own part I would be just as happy vaporized by an atomic blast as to linger on in the fallout and potentially die- and for many this would be their fate; for those in more remote areas, or areas not directly affected due to weather, their fate is more likely a positive one- but as this work explains the complications of such a war go far beyond simply a varied loss of life and a large range of radioactive contamination- the secondary loss of life would be just as egregious but can be ameliorated by a few practices which would be simplistic even after the war.

There is an interesting work called "War's End" by Wing Anderson which compiles part of a prophetic poem written by Cudmore in 1899 long before the atomic era:

> "...From fire and smoke great will be the gloom
> It may be perhaps the day of doom."

Truer words never were penned despite the religious overtones of the prophecy, which only failed if you pair it with Anderson's predictions regarding the second world war. As for the third which is to come, we can say neither one way nor the other.

WHY NUCLEAR WAR IS INEVITABLE

When most people regard the odds of a nuclear war they look to the doomsday clock (currently three minutes to midnight- an especially bad reading which itself may be too optimistic) or to analysis which treats various acts and posturings of various nations as adding to some presumably small overall threat of annihilation. These acts, speeches, figures, and breaches of world order are cobbled together in an arbitrary way and then a supposedly mathematical prediction is made; predictions which have to be presumed at least somewhat inaccurate because there is no preceding real world comparison where such a war occurred.

Rather, when I say nuclear was is inevitable, I say this because instead of looking at what may cause a nuclear war, I look instead at *what may prevent it.* This, I say, is why it will happen- because there is no scenario capable of preventing a nuclear war which wouldn't either be temporary, or reversed, or fail altogether.

Let us look at what some very well meaning but delusional folks say today- that the world should disarm itself, that nuclear states ought to forgo nuclear armaments. A laudable goal, to say the least. These individuals are a laughably small minority because most pragmatists have come to a similar conclusion to the one I espouse; disarmament is impossible. Now it remains to speak of why it is so.

Let us envision disarmament. Let us say all nuclear states give their nuclear weapons up and destroy them. Very well, the world is safe.

Or is it?

Let us now say, that some years later, or perhaps centuries, a war erupts. There are no nuclear weapons to prevent wars anymore, and they will likely become more frequent as long-simmering old scores are settled. The world might destabilize utterly and devolve into a repeat of the second world war, only far more vast. Small nations with the will and ability will attack other nations for land, having hit carrying capacity. Powerful nations will oppress the weaker, and everyone in so doing such things will then come to one conclusion; they need nuclear weapons.

Woe unto the world should the disarmament crowd actually disarm the nations of their missiles, because in the fury that follows, nations will likely conglomerate together into several poles and rip each other apart, then develop nuclear weapons all over again and deploy them, destroying large swaths of land- here the world has suffered even more than if they had just kept the weapons to begin with- paradoxical since lack of disarmament implies inevitable use of such weapons, for they would not exist if the will to use them was not present; some states *have* disarmed because they lacked such will. South Africa and Brazil are notable- the former had such weapons, the latter a sort of exploratory development program. Neither have nuclear weapons anymore.

Disarmament will land us back where we are right now, only less stable because perhaps more trigger-happy nations will have developed nuclear weapons, since there would be no nuclear states to threaten them with annihilation if they tried. Any halfway organized state can develop such weapons, and they can do it secretly if they know how- more nations in this world are capable of developing at least primitive atomic weapons than are not- North Korea has them, Israel has them, the Saudi Arabians probably have them, and even a nation like India is able to boost the fission thereof and turn twenty kilotons into two hundred kilotons with a concerted effort and without permission because they already have the weapons to resist attempts at containing such programs.

Now let us say that instead of disarmament (which I have explained is ultimately impossible) things stay the same- geopolitically stagnant and armed with nuclear weapons. Is it not just a matter of time before sabotage or accident causes a weapon, or a lot of weapons, to be fired? And what of the dead hand, or similar automated systems should such a nation be attacked? Saboteurs could detonate a single atomic warhead in Moscow, killing every Russian politician such that the dead hand is activated by soldiers who may be totally unawares that the west did not attack the Russians, they may then fire thousands of missiles, and get the same in return, all because of one saboteur. It would be asinine to think the western nuclear states do not have similar programs- the British have something similar for their submarine based warheads.

Now let us take into consideration the breakdown of mutually assured destruction (MAD). For decades, the idea that any nuclear states attacking each other causes both to be utterly destroyed has *prevented* the offensive use of nuclear weapons as well as biological and chemical ones. As such nuclear states do not attack one another, and if they desired to cause mayhem would use proxy states to fight for them instead against the allies of the other nuclear state, as we see in the middle east right now.

MAD breaks down when one of several things happens, and its protective barrier to nuclear exchange is thus removed simultaneously.

First, a nuclear state may develop technology making retaliatory strikes from another nuclear state ineffective, blocking most or all missile, sub, or jet based atomic weapons.

Second, a major nuclear state may destabilize, leaving the status of its weapons stockpile in doubt. Other states may attempt to intercede or may not.

Third, two or more nuclear states may end up exchanging non-nuclear blows. When it becomes clear one or both sides are not willing to use nuclear weapons, the system of MAD has broken down at least in that specific conflict. Say, Pakistan and India come to blows, and upon nuclear arming, one or both never actually fire the missiles or send out the jets.

Fourth, a nuclear state may be unable to continue maintaining its stockpile- the half life of some designs' warheads mean they eventually become unable to undergo fission.

Fifth, regime change, social change, or some other process may find a nuclear state taken over by those of a generally pacifistic nature, which then demand such weapons be done away with.

The first possibility looms as we speak- the United States has already successfully tested a sort of weapon- a ship-mounted laser system- with astonishing accuracy and power. Were such systems deployed on and around the borders of all NATO states it is conceivable that Russia and possibly other states, not willing to risk being surrounded and unable to ever break free, will attack preemptively, at least on a limited scale. Likewise, were Russia to suddenly attempt to deploy tens of thousands of antimissile and anti-air batteries around Russia and its allies, it is conceivable that the United States or some other state may attempt to do the same. At the very least it would be a new arms race- not a race for better weapons but rather better defense from the weapons of the other side. For this purpose *even strictly defensive advances could cause a nuclear war.* Non-weapons meant to be deployed only against aggressive targets encroaching on territorial soil could be just as paranoia-inducing as offensive systems.

So I say, nuclear war is inevitable. With disarmament impossible (long term) and with the risk of accidents or espionage, as well as the far broader issue of proliferation (India, Pakistan, North Korea, and Israel all developed their nuclear systems outside of normal treaties and protocols) combined with the inevitable breakdown of MAD, such an event is held off solely by the will and rationale of individuals within military bodies and governments. That most of these individuals see war as a profit-making endeavor is not particularly comforting. Far worse, some of them are as bitterly aggressive as possible on all sides and a great many individuals in every nuclear state would hardly want to miss a chance to catch the foe when they're somehow weak, crippled, or disarmed, so that they can lay waste to them and claim a victory after what sometimes amounts to decades of stalemate, as between Russia and the United States, or Israel and some of its neighbors, or which could occur on the Korean Peninsula.

There is a further concern. When we observe the first two world wars, they were both *caused* by alliance and politicking, rather than prevented by them. The complicated web of alliances and economic ties of the world today do not bode well, should any nuclear state attack any of its neighbors. Here is another paradox and we see it in the modern state of Russia in recent years with Ossetia in Georgia and parts of Ukraine, specifically the Crimean peninsula.

In both cases, the Russian state saw fit to essentially invade and annex foreign soil from non nuclear states. The latter is more concerning for there was a technical treaty in place which had been in place whereby Ukraine gave up its nuclear weapons to Russia at large in return for a guarantee of protection. This guarantee as, thus far, not been honored.

Thus, all nuclear states face the inevitable decision in the case where another nuclear nation becomes a warmonger and seeks to expand; do they defend their non nuclear allies and risk atomic war, or do they balk at the notion, stand back and wage proxy wars (usually fated to fail) while funding and arming smaller forces doomed to be usurped by the warmongering nuclear state? The outcome, should levels of paranoia and concern rise high enough, is the same regardlcss of their decision; nuclear war could begin at any time because of a miscalculation by either side. Such miscalculations have only by sheer chance been avoided several times already, most recently in the 1990s with a certain missile testing in Scandinavia that sent the Kremlin into uproar, and prior to that in the United States where a training program had accidentally been played on actual working defense systems, making a large number of people worry that Russia had fired large numbers of missiles at the United States without any warning. A single phone call put both issues to rest, but the age of paranoia we're in now is no less dangerous than the one we were all in during the 1980s and is approaching Cuban Missile Crisis proportions; a period in which a submarine armed with nuclear weapons was very nearly fired upon, which would likely have caused worldwide doom.

In the case of disarmament, unlike with other options, we might also expect the rise of something perhaps arguably more insidious than even MAD itself.

Let us look to the past. The United States had nuclear weapons for several years without any other power obtaining them- only when the Soviets obtained working designs from the Rosenbergs were they able to deploy their own atomic weapons. In that span of time, General Patton and others desired to attack Russia- but this left the US in a bind, because the use of nuclear weapons against Russia would have been a moral nightmare (there was already backlash from their deployment in Japan, and also with the firebombing of Dresden in Germany, which killed tens of thousands of civilians in a firestorm.) Invading without them would have been costly even if a coalition was built, and the European states were in no mood for another major campaign.

Cool heads prevailed- but if we imagine a scenario of disarmament we may imagine a future where whoever first develops working weapons the next time around is *not* swayed by pacifism and deploys them on other states attempting to develop such systems. In this case we could see the rise of a near invincible state which lords over all others in a singular-poled world, not in a benevolent manner but a malevolent one, slowly depopulating all resistance and claiming more and more land. Indeed this happens even without nuclear weapons on the table.

There was some degree of awe affecting the world when the supposedly warmongering Ronald Reagan, during his debate with Walter Mondale, suggested he would give the Soviets technology to bring down all nuclear weapons, should the US develop it first. When we look at the logic here we can say there could have been two reasons he stated this, especially when he was seen as the great anti-communist grandfather of American moral fiber.

The first possibility is that he meant it- he foresaw what I foresee; which is that only continuing MAD can save us all from nuclear armageddon. This technology transfer to the Soviets would at once reduce paranoia substantially while preventing them from attempting preemptive strikes, if such systems were deployed.

The second is that he foresaw that it would greatly increase paranoia on the other side if he did not at least *say* he intended to do so. By stating this, he put the onus on the Soviets to come to the table or risk looking violent by comparison with a man who internally had no intent to give such systems until they were already ready to deploy en masse, thus playing a few mind games with a foe which he calculated would not fire their own weapons in a situation where the intent of the US was vague, and would wait until it was *certain* what the intent was. Even in this situation it simply kicks the can down the road to armageddon though; let us remember that it would barely matter if the missiles were all brought down, because fallout alone would be severe and worldwide and affect non nuclear states as well.

PRAY THAT IT HAPPENS IN WINTER

Unfortunately only one half of the planet is in winter at a time- if it's cold and snowy in my native New England, it's a nice sunny day in Australia. Thankfully for those in Southern latitudes, the bulk of nuclear weapons, nuclear states, and thus nuclear targets are in the Northern hemisphere- in fact, there are *no nuclear weapons in the Southern hemisphere at all.* Fallout levels will be considerably lower in these areas of the world, should a nuclear exchange happen. Rejoice, Argentina, you're in about the safest spot on Earth. Perhaps we might make a rather religious statement here about the meek inheriting the planet.

Should a nuclear war erupt during the winter in the Northern hemisphere the world will be spared at least a portion of its misery- the blasts will be the same, the death toll from the explosions the same also- however the fallout will *not* behave in the same manner. Specifically, in areas with large snowfall, a lot of that radioactive ash will sit on the surface of the snow rather than penetrate otherwise penetrable soil. When the thaw comes, a great deal of it will run off into waterways and out to sea, rather than soak into soil that is still frozen for days or even weeks after the snow has melted. Because of the near impermeability of frozen soil, the contamination level on land would be far lower if a nuclear war erupts in winter time. Anyone in any nuclear states' government who warmongers ever more for such a war should at least spare us the widespread contamination of our agricultural lands so the human race can rebuild.

Thus, with only a few inches of contamination-contamination of a reduced nature to begin with- it would be far quicker for the human race to return to normal. It is also conceivable that marginally agricultural areas around bomb epicenters would be shielded from the soil there being "glassed" since the snow would absorb the seconds-long burst of radiation, melting away and carrying the radioactivity as well into sewage systems and again into waterways. While this morbidly insane release of radioactive contamination would surely poison these waterways and reduce oceanic life, it would leave the soil arable within mere weeks.

The presence of snow would perhaps also reduce the firestorm effect, as it melts and slowly inundates surrounding areas. Λ roof covered in snow will not explode into flame and become a charred layer of blackened soot very easily. In nuclear tests, even a layer of white paint sometimes prevented a fire, or at least slowed its ignition enough to conceivably allow the homeowner (if still alive- that is, not in the actual blast zone) to slosh a bucket of water over any live cinders. Snow is white and highly reflective (as I myself know from experiencing pre-snowblindness after sunny winter days shoveling the driveway.) It is protective. Its presence would dilute and ameliorate radioactivity and possibly damage to structures. Any little help would be welcome by anyone in such a situation.

Russia, perpetually snowbound as it is in winter, and the United States also being the same, a nuclear war in winter would see at least some proportion of the radioactivity leeched off the soil by melting snow. This would also be the case should China become involved, or France, although the ever-foggy Britain might not see substantial enough snow for this to be the case- in the British Isles the (rather large) coastal regions experience snowfall which is substantially lower than that of, say, Siberia or the Northern half of the states. For India and Pakistan, snowfall in the lower regions is infrequent, and tends to be more prevalent in higher mountain ranges or in the Northernmost parts of both states- in any case the population density in urban zones in both states is extreme and the destabilization resulting from such a war would be incalculably severe. As for Israel and its neighbors in the desert, much of their soil is sterile, and snowfall rare. The Korean Peninsula experiences a great deal of cold, however.

The general fallout pattern would also be changed. Here in my native New England, winter air tends to come down from sparsely populated sub-arctic regions in Canada- which would preclude at least some fallout, since there would likely be few targets here to strike, but in summer the air can come from below, from far more densely populated coastal regions, or from the west, where a large number of military installations could be targeted. It is up to the reader to determine likely wind directions and thus a rudimentary idea of fallout movement.

DON'T BOTHER EVACUATING

Often we get the idea that evacuating urban zones is a good idea- specifically because the average person presumes that the foe would target population centers in an effort to crush the enemy and prevent them from ever mobilizing for any form of counterattack. Both the US and Russia have doctrines which seemingly state they will not target civilian centers and would be more worried about trying to strike ICBM sites and other military locations. This may or may not be a genuine doctrine- it could also be a public message that would be entirely forsaken were an actual nuclear exchange to take place. There is a great deal of ambiguity in such doctrines.

However if one side attacks preemptively, the other would almost surely attack the civilian centers of the other, as a form of collective revenge against a nation which has gone rogue- again as before it matters little if the threat is perceived or real, and it matters little what some international law says about genocide when missiles are being fired that are capable of destroying everything for miles in any direction. Especially with the notoriously inaccurate systems of less developed states, the capacity may not even exist to properly aim the ICBMs, as air-based bombs would be shot down more easily than missiles traveling at far higher speeds.

As such, evacuating makes no sense for a whole host of reasons, not least of which being the foe could miss your city only to hit the outlying area you have taken refuge in.

Since it is not possible to determine ahead of time what targets might specifically be fired upon, or how accurate the barrage would be, it makes more sense to just hope you don't get hit and shelter in place unless you have substantial prior warning- say a few hours, whereby you can reliably get miles away from any possible target. Otherwise you may have as little as a few minutes' warning, or depending on circumstances, possibly none at all- an enemy nation could deploy an EMP device and knock out most communications systems within the defending nation, thus preventing most citizens from thinking anything has happened other than a routine power outage unless they were close enough to see the EMP itself courtesy of a thermonuclear device detonated miles above their heads.

Additionally, evacuation whether ordered or not would be a haphazard panic of fleeing vehicles and pedestrians- in this death trap you might expect a large number of casualties before the warheads have even fallen; death that is all that much more ironic when you consider the possibility that any ordinance aimed at the city itself may not even impact close enough to it to cause substantial damage; it could be that some such weapons don't even detonate at all and simply lay there, panicking bystanders as they wonder if it will suddenly go off, killing everyone for a mile around at some random time.

Unless a substantial advance notice is given, evacuation is pointless.

Additionally, following a nuclear war, order will break down. Perhaps it will only be crippled and remnants of order will remain, or perhaps the destruction will be so great as to render all modes of control useless except at exceedingly local levels- say, a sheriff who manages to rally a village of fifty people so that they can reorganize afterward- extremely rural areas would be likely to recover more quickly unless directly in the path of severe fallout.

Since order will have broken down, and because everyone will be in a paranoid fight-or-flight mode, infighting could break out, and it would be far easier for any person able to defend themselves to do so on their own terms, in an area they are used to being in, with whatever weapons they may possess. I here submit that any citizen who doesn't have at least one firearm is an absolute fool, not because they are routinely necessary in day to day life but because such things will not be good but rather *necessary for survival* in a post-atomic world, if only for fending off scavenging, mutated animals covered in blistering sores that will act violently specifically because they are crippled and in pain. Packs of feral dogs will roam the countryside and cities, and this is a perfect storm as well for rabies and other pestilence. In further chapters I will explain things related to this concept. Your firearm need not be a high caliber armor-piercing death machine, a simple .22 revolver and a few boxes of bullets is enough for the outbreak of feral animals that will be a far, far greater threat than vandals, gangs, or foreign invasion, at least in most areas for a substantial time after the war.

If we assume that everyone evacuates every city and town, most of them will have done so in vain- there are not enough nuclear weapons possessed by any state to directly impact and destroy more than a large minority of metropolitan areas in any other, likely hostile nation, with the exception of, say, Russia going after France or Britain, or the US suddenly attacking North Korea, or something of that nature- rather, in a full exchange we can expect the major nuclear states to fling their payloads at not one but *numerous* nations- essentially all non-allied nations, and all other nuclear states not directly in their sphere of friendship. The United States would not attack France or Britain, but it would be *likely* to hurl missiles at China despite amicable trade relations. Russia would not fire on Belarus or Kazakhstan, but it would be *likely* to at least target the capitols of various non-nuclear states in Europe, even though they would be unable to fight back against such an assault. If India and Pakistan were to use nuclear weapons, it is likely China would be involved, and possibly Iran as well, because contamination ignores national borders.

This is all theoretical; the main point is that the nukes will be spread fairly thin because multiple nations will be targeted. Yes, the lion's share may be reserved specifically for one especially powerful enemy, but your town of 50,000 people is rather *unlikely* to be deliberately targeted. For most people, the threat is not being vaporized, but rather suffering from fallout, the breakdown of order, contamination leading to famine, secondary outbreaks of disease, and possible invasion by foreign or domestic militant elements.

THE MINIMALIST SURVIVAL CHECKLIST

Although extremely elaborate survivalist gear and planning is available, most people lack the interest or money necessary to acquire them. As such, this is a stripped down checklist of some goods which ought to be obtained by anyone that intends to survive, should atomic war come into use.

First, iodine. One of the more short-lived but dangerous isotopes created by nuclear weapons is an isotope of this thyroid-absorbed element; thankfully for the human race, the thyroid soaks up regular, non-radioactive iodine preferentially, and only a deficiency of natural iodine will cause it to absorb any quantity of the radioactive kind in fallout. A two week course of potassium iodide pills will prevent most cases of thyroid cancer that would otherwise result from exposure.

Second, a firearm and ammunition. As I stated it is *not* necessary that this weapon be particularly ferocious, although you can obtain whatever you think suits you. Hopefully you know how to actually use it- both fire it and maintain it, that is, with some degree of confidence. I say not necessary for it to be particularly ferocious, because you are far more likely to need it to kill feral dogs or rabid wild animals or to defend yourself against a lightly armed adversary than you are to need it to cut down lines of soldiers covered head to toe in body armor wielding machine guns.

Third, water. Potable water- this is more important than food and for some time after the war most water would be contaminated. You can obtain filtration systems that will remove some radioactive materials- alpha particles mainly, and which will also remove parasites- but it is just as easy to have some water on hand before such an event. In the case of an EMP water systems will be debilitated in some areas, so having at least a few gallons of water on hand would be ideal, and you can store far more than that if you wish.

Fourth, food. Specifically food in sealed containers. A ten gallon plastic bucket can be used to store a great deal of food- at least a month's supply is ideal, of dried, salted, candied, or canned foods. If the food is canned you will, of course, want to have a can opener (so as to avoid an extremely funny but frustrating post-apocalyptic self deprecation.)

Fifth, basic medical supplies- a first aid kit and perhaps something more; specifically because the medical system will have been annihilated. Nothing would be worse than surviving a nuclear war and then being killed by tetanus or gangrene weeks later.

Sixth, a gas mask and filters to be used for some time after the war. The filters cannot be 1990s era surplus- these amusingly contain elements that decay and become mildly radioactive themselves, and modern filters are readily available.

Seventh, seeds. Lots of them- heirloom and non GMO, so that you can gather your own seed from plants left unharvested. Greens, fruits, and especially legumes with some sort of grain (preferably flint corn for meal and hominy, or else wheat.)

Optionally you can obtain any other weapons, ammunition, food, construction materials for fortifying a location, and most especially *anything which can produce electricity.* If an EMP is released, homes powered by solar panels within the blast will be useless, as the panels will likely short out, but stored panels which are not yet installed will be at a premium, as will anything producing wind power, and as will gas generators and gas.

This checklist is *extremely* minimalistic. Some people have a years' supply of food, a whole stock of guns and ammo, and plenty of seeds to replant after the nuclear holocaust- this sort of setup requires more planning and money to put into use.

A Geiger counter is also an extremely good idea- as would at least one hazmat suit or similar coverall to prevent contamination of clothing and body. We must remember that there are different types of radioactivity- alpha emitters are virtually harmless externally but will do immense damage if ingested, while beta emitters are more harmful to be around in general without ingestion (and the latter is what is typically tested for by counters at contaminated sites.) The reader is reminded that in the wake of total social breakdown, nuclear plants (at least those of the older variety) will surely melt down and contamination will be vastly increased downwind of these plants.

DISPOSAL OF CORPSES AND DETRITUS

After the nuclear exchange, should you be within an area impacted by fire or fallout, one of the primary tasks that will be necessary to perform is the removal of the dead and of various waste that will certainly be present- even in a rural area, contaminated waste will be everywhere- essentially any compacted, decaying leaves, branches, grass, and so forth on the surface of the ground, and in urban areas, trash of various sorts. Outside of destroyed areas there may be miles of partly ruined material, with bricks and steel and glass everywhere- these blighted zones will nonetheless be habitable if cleaned. Corpses in the latter areas will be plentiful.

Let us consider the manner of the corpses. Bodies near the impact zones will probably be charred and crispy- they will be too carbonized and radioactive to decay quickly, but thankfully these cooked corpses will also take longer to begin to rot, in the absence of significant moisture, as firestorm dries the area into carbonized wreckage. There will be at least some bloated bodies anywhere from general panic, infighting, and disease immediately after the war ends.

If you are able to do so, check the corpses for radiation. Radioactive bodies should be sealed and disposed of while sealed into a bag or plastic coffin. Burning the corpses may be necessary, but if removal is possible without doing so they ought to be buried- burning a radioactive corpse will merely scatter the radioactivity around and they must be disposed of before cholera sets in.

Standing water should be drained if possible, impact zones should be avoided and will be far more radioactive. Debris should be cleared away and buried- or sealed and buried if the capacity to do so exists. You will likely see all manner of grotesque horrors- burned bodies, dead children, dead pregnant women, mangled animals, bodies crushed by debris- be aware of any counterparts and their mental state. Do not let someone on the edge of lunacy continue to work in such conditions, but remove them to somewhere where the horror is less pronounced.

After fallout the topsoil will be contaminated (even if it had been frozen at the time of the war) to a greater or lesser degree. If the contamination is very slight leave it alone, if the contamination is moderate to severe, the following chapter will instruct the reader on ameliorating this soil condition.

Starving animals will be everywhere and will filter into formerly settled zones to feast upon the corpses. Animals which had been indoors may escape through windows or damaged sections of homes. Zoo animals may also escape if the fences are damaged- you may see exotic beasts wandering the land and these could be exceptionally dangerous. While unlikely, we might imagine that a pride of lions begins wandering around Southern Texas, or that a tiger population takes root in the Everglades. Destroy these animals if possible, retaining them only if obviously not diseased, obviously friendly, and obviously capable of being commanded for their own safety.

Cats, however, despite the risk of rabies, should *not* be destroyed. They will severely reduce any resurgent rodent populations which, after such a war, will pour out of the now disused sewers of every metropolitan area, gorging on corpses and spilled food, rapidly multiplying. Their numbers will decrease over time as they exhaust their food sources and as additional food is properly secured, but for the time being, cats ought to be left alone or even protected for use as a feral rodent extermination force. This fantastic situation is all that much funnier because of modernity's seeming resurgent cat worship-lite style of regarding them as harmless and adorable; but to a rat or mouse they are a gigantic and vehement predator. As for rabies, many cats will have been vaccinated and will be, at least in the short term, protected from such pestilence.

After the first winter most of the exotic animals will die or migrate to the warmest zones of any nation which may have been impacted- feral dogs will continue to be the worst problem and may interbreed with coyote or wolf populations, and such hybrids are far more aggressive than wolves or coyotes on their own (which are generally reclusive and avoid contact with humans out of habit.) Urban zones which had been giant game preserves for the first year will be partly depopulated, but ruined areas will become a haven for dogs. We see this already in ruined areas in places like Detroit- a cold city which nonetheless has a massive population of feral canines because there are so many structures for them to reside in and plenty of detritus to feed upon.

Those with the capacity to do so will need to organize and hunt the local feral population to bring numbers under control- otherwise they will of necessity exhaust their resources, starve, and become disease prone. A small population of feral animals will tend to remain somewhat healthier than one approaching the area's carrying capacity. From urban ruins they will spread, and soon certain domesticated species (which have become wild) will breed in the wild as well- we may envision a population of Dobermans or Rottweilers taking root in some suburban outlands and replicating there. If the population appears more gregarious (friendly) it will not be as much a pressing issue as a population which shows signs of aggression- there is a demonstrable difference between a few beagles and a horde of wolf-hybrids which lurks around thc cdges of a human settlement raiding waste. In time, should starvation set in (as it does from time to time) the stressed population may become more prone to violence. Likewise, human populations do the same, and groups of survivors are urged to form larger organization before this happens, so that infighting is reduced and the capacity of waste removal restored.

Human waste, if possible, should also be properly disposed of. If it must be burned it must be burned but human urine is mildly fertile and can be added in small amounts to various crops. Human excrement of the solid variety tends to be useless unless the population has adopted vegetarianism- this would be laudable since radioactivity will concentrate in meat at higher levels because contamination is continuously accrued and absorbed by carnivores.

Because water systems will leech radioactivity over time, aquatic food sources are more questionable than those on land- agriculture on land will remain the staple source of any food supply, at lower levels of contamination. Deep sea fishing will presumably be impossible for some time, and inland waterways such as streams and ponds and lakes will probably be more heavily contaminated by radioactivity. Thankfully, most of these isotopes will decay within a few decades and most of the contamination by then even in worse-hit areas will have substantially fallen. Only the first two or so generations will have to deal with a world which is substantially worse than at times in the pre-industrial but nonetheless civilized eras of times past.

When areas have been cleared, structures may be renovated or else destroyed for materials- wood for heating or construction and stone for the same. Bricks can be quarried as easy material to create walls or raised beds for agriculture- which will as I point out perhaps be a small-scale but important source of less contaminated food. Specifically for children and pregnant women, contamination *must* be reduced to as low a rate as possible. Bagged compost will be less contaminated if applied after active fallout has largely ended- this reduces the likelihood of birth defects. Crops grown in such raised beds- bordered by bricks or stones and filled with formerly sealed stratum- will be perfect for growing things specifically to be ingested by the young and pregnant, to reduce morbidity.

The resources available for quick access will far exceed the population in most regions. With a high death rate and plenty of less radioactive ruins left from abandonment and secondary damage, there should be relatively little competition for the basic resources necessary to sustain life. After the black death, Europe entered the Renaissance, and a relative age of peace and prosperity, specifically because there was now an excess of arable but fallow land able to be farmed by anyone willing to lay claim- as such, feudal peasantry was replaced by what may be seen as the rudiments of a middle class; former peasants or merchants who abandoned their lifestyle to farm on their own. At this time, diversification of crops begins, and mortality begins to fall because of various advances and a healthier lifestyle.

This will be offset by radioactive contaminants driving birth defects, cancers, and other forms of mortality up in rate- however the contamination will not last forever, and areas which have been scrubbed down to some degree will be habitable. It is preferable that, if possible, those decontaminating anything wear a mask and suit if they can, and homes and other structures which the population intends for living space should be thoroughly hosed down externally until the area is inundated, allowing contamination to run off into still-working sewers, or into culverts. Maintaining drainage to remove contamination through nature itself will be important as well- backed-up culverts would inundate surrounding areas with mud and drive contaminants to the surface.

SOIL RESTORATION AND AGRICULTURE

The post atomic world will require essentially the same basis for humanity as the world before the war- the main difference being that a great many cities will lie in dust and most agriculturally fertile land will contain some degree of (ever decreasing) contamination. Those worried about a Chernobyl style future of massive exclusion zones need to understand that there is a fairly large distinction between a nuclear weapon (wherein much radioactive material is rapidly decayed, releasing gamma rays) and a meltdown (wherein no nuclear explosion occurs and burning radioactive rubble releases highly contaminated smoke and steam for years or decades unless buried outright, as at Chernobyl.) Unless a meltdown has occurred within proximity, most agricultural land will be just fine and there are several ways to decontaminate it.

The first is the stripping of topsoil- the uppermost later of soil will be the most contaminated and can be removed and bagged. This is extensive work and would be quite time consuming.

There are experimental means by which some radioactive materials can be filtered- zeolite has been mentioned specifically because it contains micropores- its addition to contaminated sites can leech the radioactive materials right out of them if this act is performed properly. However there is a far easier method to construct a decontaminating matrix, as opposed to zeolite.

I speak of course of terra preta. This cure-all soil is impregnated with charcoal which has been powdered and added to it. The miniscule cellular matrix continues to function much as when the material was alive (charcoal being anaerobically cooked woody material, usually hardwood logs split into smaller sections.) This same matrix, which can retain fertilizer and moisture, and which drains excess moisture away, also reduces erosion and increases yield and soil pH balance. The addition of powdered charcoal and composted vegetation to soil following any atomic event has several purposes.

First, it will reduce the necessity of chemical fertilizers, which will be in short supply and high demand.

Second, it will help to prevent famine by specifically increasing the likelihood that a yield will be garnered, as it reduces pests and certain soil-based diseases, especially (in my experience) those affecting greens and root crops.

Third, the matrix of carbonized cell wall could potentially trap radioactive materials, preventing it from leeching into the crops themselves, reducing mutations and increasing the edibility of the foods. This is not certain but is theoretical and based on the function of porous zeolites. Charcoal, you will note, is often used in filtration systems, where it does a great deal of good for a fraction of the price of other systems.

Soil which has been thus amended prior to fallout will be easily decontaminated- specifically because the carbon rich matrix will hold the contamination at a very thin upper layer. When we speak of contamination we must differentiate between severity thereof, because after such a war most of the world will be at least slightly dusted with radioactivity.

An area immediately adjacent to any impact, or downwind of a melted nuclear plant, will be too radioactive to inhabit. Protective clothing would need to be worn to even pass by the area safely.

An area further away will be more moderately contaminated. After decontamination is undertaken the area may or may not be habitable but it will at least be passable.

Most other areas will only see mild contamination which will have degraded to a marginally safe level after several weeks- this does not mean there will not be an ever-present higher risk of cancer and birth defects, but such a risk will exist regardless of where a person happens to be residing. Unfortunately it may be difficult to tell if an area is significantly contaminated unless one has a working Geiger counter- however anyone would know to avoid "the big steaming crater where the city used to be."

Since everything will have been touched by the fallout, any soil to be used for agriculture should be stripped of topsoil first. Areas which were fallow will see much of the radiation leeched into grass or shrubbery and this can be stripped up as well.

Now we have to consider the possibility of significant climate changes following such an event. The loss of soil cover could temporarily desertify large areas and fallout will surely kill plants at various regions even miles from any impact or meltdown. As such, dust will enter the atmosphere and may cause global cooling, extended winters, and erratic weather in general. Some crops fare better than others under such forms of abuse- it is exceptionally difficult to kill a radish or a turnip, or cabbage, but tomatoes may be in short supply.

Ultimately man tends to remain dependent on staple grains- and these should definitely be sown alongside legumes even if the latter are not eaten, to restore nitrogen to the soil which is taken up in large amount by the same grains. Far short of competing, legumes and grains compliment one another, and some legumes can be stored for long periods as a staple if dried, such as lentils or most beans. There is a native method of planting called the three sisters which adds squash plants to the mix- the squash suppresses weeds from around the roots of the legumes and grains, the grains provide a trellis for the legumes, and the legumes provide nitrogen directly as well as the subsequent off season when they die and the nitrogen built up by michhorizae on the roots is released into the soil from the root nodes where nitrogen fixing bacteria thrive. In the post atomic world, it is possible that any of these crops may be found to fail more readily, and it is not definite that nitrogen fixing bacteria will be as readily produced even on such nodes as prior to the war.

Other crops can create nitrogen as well- alfalfa can be sown as a green compost (whereby it is killed in autumn and plowed into the soil.) Clover plants also create such nitrogen in the soil, and some areas are choked with clover plants.

Raising animals is a different task altogether. Domesticated cows will die if not milked, and many other domesticated animals will die rapidly in the absence of human care, where they are fenced in. It may not make sense to raise cows for dairy to begin with since it will concentrate contamination- some radioactivity was found in milk as far away from Japan as New England, after the meltdown at Fukushima. Chickens are a better bet- the intensification of contamination in a chicken, as a much smaller animal, is lower, and the amount of resources required to produce chickens for eggs or meat is far less than for beef, pork, or other larger animals. Chickens are also easier to deal with and require less general working knowledge, whereas cows can be cantankerous. Chickens provide the added benefit of being birds, and thus not getting rabies.

Wild game will be everywhere but every wild animal should be considered a potential health threat due to disease and contamination. Presume that any wild animal not known to you is either sick or contaminated from scavenging radioactive garbage. If you are starving, this will obviously not be an impediment to consuming it.

Certain photosynthetic life could become particularly valuable. Birch wood, especially paper birch which is common in some Northern areas, will burn even when green, providing easy fuel for fires. Wild berries and various medicinal plants grow across the world. Here I cannot provide a guide to these plants, because the reader may not be in an area where I am familiar with the local flora- instead the reader should amend this work with a relevant guide to medicinal and edible species in their nation and region.

Plants able to drive out infection due to antimicrobial and antibacterial properties will become the most valuable of all. Here in the United States witch hazel (an astringent) and white sage (with its antimicrobial properties) as well as any wild edible crops would be in vogue after such an event. Wild plants such as berries can be propagated as well, if pruning is acquired as a skill- a relatively small berry patch can provide a massive amount of food, and in rural areas foraging would at least provide a substantial ease for the need to work feverishly to grow domesticated crops.

Certain insects rely upon magnetic fields for navigation- atomic war would severely disturb the life cycle of the world, suddenly destroying most electronics and perturbing the world's magnetic field itself with EMP blasts- I cannot theorize as to what effect this may have upon migratory birds and most flying insects but we can presume it would be a negative effect.

FORTIFICATIONS AND SELF DEFENSE

When nuclear annihilation is depicted in movies, the survivors typically end up amalgamating into tribe-like groups and squabbling over land and resources. This would be a fairly unlikely scenario, since the amount of land available would be in excess of the amount required to sustain the much-reduced population of any area suffering significant instability. Self defense is still key, though, if only because starving, scavenging animals might come calling and raid crops or hen houses, or attack humans out of desperation. Here I will regard also a simple concept; any standing force in the world intent upon attacking and invading affected regions will necessarily use certain tactics and have certain gear for doing so- if such a force even exists after the world economy declines back to the levels of the 1800s.

It is far more likely that the reader will need to deal with the unavailability of a few key goods rather than land; and where there is land, food may be produced, as long as effort is undertaken to do so. Survivalists and rural agrarian folks will continue to work their fields, but may or may not have a reliable surplus to dole out to others regardless of what goods may be offered in trade for the same. It will be up to each individual or group to defend themselves and obtain the rudiments of life, and any fighting occurring between people from the same overall culture is an exceptionally bad idea, because the population will already be under severe stress. Fighting, thus, should be discouraged if possible, and only be undertaken if necessary.

Organization is a far better strategy- specifically loose organization, as in proximity and general shared culture rather than a group of humans surrounding any sort of leader or figurehead- a group which has thus loosely organized itself (preferably in agreement over a general set of rules and a constitution) will prevail where disorganized remnants fall into chaos. If two groups fight, there may be casualties, and both groups are thus weakened, and less able to respond to a more objective threat, such as foreign invasion, famine, epidemic, or other disaster. This ought to be kept in mind, should two groups argue over a resource, location, or philosophical concept.

Those who find themselves alone will be best served by fortifying whatever location they have already inhabitcd unlcss it is burned or significantly damaged- the individual in such a case has a knowledge of their surroundings and habitation which others which may come knocking do not necessarily have. From a mental standpoint, continuing to inhabit your same home brings about at least a facade of normalcy, and even flimsy homes may be fortified fairly easily. Fencing and loose wood or other material to construct additional fencing will be plentiful in many areas, as will materials for buffing up the walls, replacing windows or roofing, and so forth. There is an additional reason to stay put if able; even a seemingly abandoned home may be only temporarily so, with the family once living there returning in force- and should they find you therein, they may believe you constitute a threat and thus fire first and ask questions later. Better to lay low and observe for some time before making such a switch as needed.

A group has more options because they have more manpower to gather and deploy materials. Weapons may be freely available or may not be, but it is a simple effort to fence off a building (or more than one if the need arises.) This fencing wouldn't normally be a deterrence to even a small force of men should they be armed, but in the post atomic world, the fuel necessary for even a substantial foreign army to field tanks and other vehicles will be tenuous at best- as such any such fighting force is likely to be somewhat confused in what may be new surroundings, and may as well be on foot. Something as simple as a single lamp or a single fireplace sending smoke up the chimney may be able to attract attention, but then you simply have to take stock of what types of things may be attracted to your habitation. The individual or group will have to determine whether any arrivals are to be trusted or not.

A location which was heavily built to begin with- say a large stone structure with an outer wall- will be far easier to defend than the average home, which may be quite close to nearby homes and have a relatively small area which is arable. Any structure to be requisitioned may still have some electricity going to it- downed power lines should still be considered a hazard, potentially. Solar cells, wind fields, and generators will continue to feed power into the lines, and although these areas of electricity may be sporadic, anything near to them may contain downed but live wires and other associated power hazards.

Larger organized groups may construct more elaborate fortifications out of even scrap material- vehicles can be used to block roads in general areas. We might consider, for example, a cul de sac which has been fenced off, with only one entrance by road- with the road partly blocked and a "gate" created using either fencing or perhaps a vehicle which still works, which can be used to selectively block movement- while this is hardly an air tight system it will discourage looters and animals.

In the third world, specifically areas of it with little to no actual development, life will continue as it did before amongst those capable of raising or otherwise obtaining food- however some third world regions have been, for a time now, reliant on aid from the first world; especially medical aid and food surplus shipments. Famine will almost surely set in, as will epidemic- these diseases, once they are able to take hold, will then spread by trade should it still exist- in such areas, fortification is less necessary than access to clean water and safe food supplies.

It is almost certain that a proportion of the populations will have become lunatics owing to the sheer horror of seeing cities turned to ashes. As such we may expect the occasional reclusive hermit in the deeper sections of the radioactive wastes left behind from bombed out cities. We might also expect the occasional violent cannibal or criminal madman who has reverted to animalism. The former is best left alone, the latter are best avoided or, if impossible, destroyed.

Areas which afford some view of surrounding regions will be especially valuable- say the roof of a taller building in what's left of a city, or a hill, or even a tower, as they exist in some regions; here in New England, the remains of various woolen mills from the bygone industrial boom of the late 1800s and early 1900s, would afford excellent spots to see in some cases for miles in every direction- so too would mountain villages be of value, or certain buildings in some of our larger towns. The likelihood that any of these regions would be purposely targeted is low due to the exceedingly low population density in even our largest city, and most cities of any size are far away making even an accidental impact less likely- however these buildings come with the drawbacks of cold weather- mountains would become impassable due to lack of maintenance to the roads, and century-old mill towers are flimsy at best. As for taller buildings, it would require a substantial amount of effort to properly guard and maintain such a structure, though it can surely be done.

Those with experience in masonry, carpentry, architecture, engineering, and other mechanical sciences or skilled trades would be invaluable- not only for their own work but their ability to teach it to others. An organized group which actively encourages its members to learn at least the basics of such abilities will find it far easier to defend themselves- perhaps easier even than a group taking up a more militaristic mindset and training everyone to kill. The latter could get stranded in the wilderness and experience severe attrition while the former, otherwise less well defended, is at least not freezing to death.

So too is agriculture important- here fortification is melded with such a trade because protecting crops, if only from rogue animals, will be of highest importance. In the post-war era for some time food will be readily available in the form of canned, dried, roasted, salted, candied, and pickled materials which last for quite some time. However, even if the stock of such can last a year or more, this should be seen solely as a temporary relief from the need to farm, specifically allowing enough time to develop the means to do so later. Every day of this expanse of time should be dedicated to constructing the necessary rudiments of a city-state or fortified home or neighborhood, and to then tilling the land and preparing it for growing things.

Thus, the primary goal of an organized group in such an event should be to first obtain such food solely so they can dedicate additional time to other things- even if that consists of erecting only a short chain link fence around a few homes and then tilling five or six acres of land. Most people seem to believe it is necessary to farm hundreds of acres for only a few people- this is not the case, and modern farming fields have been made that size to develop surplus specifically for sale at profit. When the necessity is instead a smaller surplus for a smaller group the effort required is lesser. These areas to be used as such, regardless of size or crops, should be fenced at least, if not walled off. It is possible, in time, that some groups will quite literally construct walled cities- miniature city states, perhaps even fortresses, all from scrap material left in the ruins. After all the surplus material will be several orders of magnitude higher than needed for such a thing.

RESTORING ORDER

Paradoxically, while food, water, and shelter are technically more important than the presence of order, the presence of order makes obtaining (and retaining) these other facets of life far less difficult. A group, however large, working under some system of order, will tend towards a better chance of survivorship. Here I submit that the proper manner of doing so is with some sort of working constitution- any basic legal system can be implemented, but the group will function more easily if the rules are lax and loose, and organization predominantly arranged around voluntary inclusion and self-led endeavors which are voluntarily enjoined by others as they wish. For example, we might envision two groups, one led as such and one by a charismatic leader of sorts.

The group led by a denoted, dedicated leadership figure will make more progress, but only if that same leader is competent. Should they fail, the group may end up hanging them in frustration, or fracturing. Conversely, the looser group in which most acts are voluntary will be less prone to such fracturing, even if during good times they make slightly less progress- and even this is not certain, because they may themselves be competent and rational enough to make their own decisions. Let us here remember that in the wake of any nuclear war, the war will have culminated as the result of direct concerted effort by legalistic and militaristic groups led by dictators, oligarchs, and elected officials gone rogue- no sane people would undertake such an act, as to destroy their own planet.

One main philosophical tenet of any such group should simply be this; while ethnic and cultural squabbles from the past may be tempting (as in, groups may attempt to settle old scores now that the world is in wreckage), there are two reasons to ignore these old arguments and finally move past them. First, most of these arguments were formulated and artificially promulgated by the same governments that will have been responsible for the suffering of the war, and secondly now will be the time at which it is finally possible to rebuild a world in which the same struggle does not exist.

Man will always compete, and thus will always find disagreements arising over resources and land, but in this new world land is free to anyone and resources far in excess of the amount needed at least for basic survival, if not virtually inexhaustible expansion at least until the world reaches, once again, the same population as it had before, which will take at least decades and probably centuries. These populations will already be under stress and avoiding conflict will be important to them all. The intelligent survivor will remember that the average citizen of even the most warmongering nation wanted to be left alone, and is now also likely dead because of their own government's actions.

Many areas will find themselves reduced to more or less culturally homogenous cores- small pockets of (mostly) rural individuals away from former cosmopolitan areas. The age of urbanism will decay, as it will be temporarily impossible for a city of modern size to exist.

These post-atomic survivors have one major advantage over those living in ages' past when the population was also lower than it is today, and when the world was wracked by various trouble as the result of constant war- namely that technology will be everywhere, and everything from a modern printing system to libraries filled with informational volumes will be present for exploitation. Currently, learning is seen by many as boring or dull- in the future, after such a war, this would not be the case, and it would instead be much more than a pastime and would be increasingly valuable. Those able to maintain and construct electrical equipment, and those with knowledge of medicine, will be likely the most cherished of all, and those able to grow food may be able to sustain a substantially growing, increasingly organized population.

The restoration of order to areas will fall flat if those attempting to do so predominantly rely upon force to do so. There is an old adage here that comes to mind; "You get more flies with a spoonful of sugar than a gallon of vinegar." We may expect, at least in some regions, that a lot of the prior bickering over race, religion, creed, and so forth, may fall apart primarily for the same reasons such arguments were less common in the past in parts of the Western world; people will be so focused on obtaining food and goods and bringing back some semblance of order, that they will be mostly unconcerned with the choices of others unless their choices are harmful to other human beings, or detrimental overall to the odds of survival of a group. "Don't be an idiot" could probably substitute temporarily for a whole host of laws and regulations.

There is another partial advantage of these future survivors over antiquated forebears which existed centuries ago- there will be a higher proportion of skilled individuals, especially those exhibiting mental and physical toughness, good instinct, and who are generally healthy, specifically because their ability to survive the war and its immediate aftermath will be higher than that of the general population. This will allow mankind to resist some of the worse effects of constant exposure to low-level radiation as well. We might imagine a sizable proportion of the survivors will be young or middle aged, and those with chronic conditions are unlikely to survive and perpetuate them, unless they have other abilities which allowed them to continue treating themselves, in which case their one weakness has been balanced by other strengths anyways.

In this quasi-meritocratic society, it may not even be necessary to exert force to retain or restore order, because the population will be generally composed of individuals with common sense. I will subsequently explain here a few temptations; behaviors the group may be coerced into undertaking, and then specifically refute why they should be used, even though the temptation to do so will be large.

First, as to the notion of expulsion or banishment; as the group will likely desire to use should there be individuals who have done nothing specifically violent but are clearly less able to properly exist in the post atomic world. Expelling them is essentially a death sentence; and this reduces available genes and overlooks their possible capacity to be taught skills that they *will* exceed at. The age of homogenized education is over, the age of tailored work has begun.

Second, as to the death penalty; such a thing would immediately bring back the same sort of false pragmatic views that led to the war in the first place (read; the lack of objective value of life itself.) If a person has killed in self defense, so be it, but for an organized group to cull a member for anything short of that person themselves attempting to kill others, is abominable considering what every survivor has witnessed.

Third, as to taxes and workings akin to them; while centralization at some degree in the past was potentially (although not always) efficient, centralization is a bad idea in such a destabilized world. Even storing goods in one place rather than spreading the stock around is a terrible idea since a house fire could then destroy most of your goods and knock you back in development. Centralization should be avoided, except where a communal structure has been made specifically for group purposes, say, a fort or something like that.

Fourth, as to religion; all people should be left alone in such beliefs- to make it an issue at such a time would simply drive a wedge between people and reduce their ability to properly work together. In some areas the religious composition will be homogenous, but even then individuals will disagree on specific tenets of their same religion. Organized religion will have been partially guilty, itself, of perpetuating the type of hate that led to the war, and should be discouraged. Turn the church or mosque into a hospital and it will be far more useful for those who have survived.

Fifth, as to dedicated government; The formation of a representational government is not, strictly, necessary when dealing with such a small area and small group, as the group will tend to be. In such a situation it makes far more sense to have little in the way of government at all, at least at first, centralizing only what resources are needed to maintain a defensive system geared mostly towards destroying feral animals and organizing for the purposes of treatment of the sick, burial or burning of the dead, and perhaps warding off looters which may arise. This relatively limited government should only be expanded in scope when necessary to continue order; and when it is indeed expanded, it ought to be subject to a constitution specifically delineating powers it has, to the exclusion of all others. At the end of this work a copy of the Bill of Rights is provided as a basis for readers who may be in this nation, should they choose (wisely, I believe) to continue using it as the basis of any organization they perpetuate.

Sixth, as to a military; the concentration of force and firepower in the hands of a few will be neither necessary nor laudable. Rather, all citizens of this new group ought to remain armed at least lightly at all times. Everything from boxes of ammunition and hunting rifles to automatic weapons, ballistic vests, and riot gear of every assortment will be readily available in vast amounts. All citizens of the group should requisition such materials sufficient for their own protection. However, establishment of military-style *training* will be commendable as a good idea. A sort of voluntary militia.

SCAVENGING THE RUINS

Scavenging what's left of society when it has been mostly obliterated by our governments will be a difficult but rewarding task- perhaps even a fun one, since it will be a bit like Indiana Jones style archaeology, or tomb raiding. The crippled, crumbling ruins will hold a little bit of everything, although some things have a definite shelf life. Interestingly, as with Chernobyl and its lower-than-normal decay rate, it is entirely possible that foodstuffs will take longer than normal to decay due to fallout.

While it may seem strange, books will be the most valuable objects in the world at this time short of electrical supplies and the means to maintain them- most of our population has grown accustomed to reading only digital works and many people own few if any books at all, but libraries, bookstores, and businesses will be full of handy manuals and so forth- especially those related to gardening and farming, construction and architecture, and engineering. Educational materials will also be widely available, since there will be children who will have survived and will require schooling in basic subjects. Courses such as math and science will be objectively more important than cultural studies, women's history, and holocaust studies, among others which have become the boring pass time of well meaning but clueless classes of humans who believe that the life cycle of the silk worm is of penultimate importance. This world will belong to the pragmatic.

When possible such works should be shared among members of the group unless enough copies exist for everyone to use their own; specifically because knowledge imparted to such a group will always be helpful. In modern times we have diverged and specialized labor, such that a doctor often is clueless about construction and a carpenter clueless about medicine. In this post-war world, it will be far better if everyone knows at least the basics about many skills, if not all of them; this is not as difficult as it sounds, to learn such things, when infinite time and materials will be available for hands-on learning.

Likewise, in our modern age, people have mostly grown accustomed to seeing physical labor (and most other work) as "not fun"- as a chore, as something to be avoided when able. Persistence of such an attitude will lead to the individual perishing, most often. Those averse to physical labor may however be able to dedicate themselves to other tasks; especially medicine and scavenging- the former requiring more encyclopedic effort, the latter more adventure than back breaking work. Indeed, with technology available before electricity was widespread it is possible to efficiently farm with far less effort than our ancestors did in the far past- anyone can attach netting to a scythe for grain harvesting, and it is not as difficult as some may believe to grow food, or to construct basic shelters. Since structures will need repair more than ground-up construction the job will be far simpler, so long as the individual is capable of hammering wood into place with nails.

After books, medical supplies will be naturally commendable to obtain. Unfortunately most of the best materials will be damaged or outdated- vaccines will be impossible to obtain because they will have gone unrefrigerated for some time, and most people would not be able to determine what materials may be infectious. In fact, hospitals especially should be avoided for some weeks after such a nuclear event, specifically because they may be breeding grounds for all forms of contamination. Protection should be worn when scavenging anything, but especially hospitals.

Weapons, armor, and other defense mechanisms will be everywhere. In areas where order has broken down utterly these will be quickly looted, and efforts should be made if possible to secure such goods to prevent looters and criminals from obtaining heavy weaponry such as grenades and automatic rifles, as well as combat armor. Should the military have been deployed by your nation prior to the war, armories and military bases may not even be staffed; you might think it a good idea to requisition a battle tank, but inability to fuel it will render it useless for anything other than emergency shelter. Such vehicles may be strategically positioned and their ability to move destroyed such that they can serve as safe spaces should a person need them for any length of time.

Water is important also. A home with an artesian well may be used to supply a great deal of it, assuming it is fitted with something to generate the electricity to do so. These water systems will eventually fail if not maintained, but local well-drilling businesses likely have manuals on hand for folks to learn how to do the same.

The same is true for electrical equipment. Your electric company may be abandoned but chances are some manuals for work remain, along with faraday suits for work on live wires, helmets, gloves, and so forth. It is an obvious necessity that anyone able to do so, should immediately set to work supplying electricity to their region. If some order remains the government may be able to do so, but chances are slim that this will be the case in most nations, and as such the best bet is to requisition solar panels or choose habitation which is still being fed energy from a wind farm or something of that nature. Natural gas will be available for generators, at least temporarily, as well.

Ultimately, scavenging wood will be important for heating structures as well as potentially for creating charcoal as a soil amendment. There will be no shortage since old structures can be destroyed for their framing, and most of the world contains some level of forest cover. Trees should be cut and split properly, and replanting efforts undertaken, although forests will quickly begin to take over what were once cities, at least in some areas.

In fact, as we see with disturbed areas and with abandoned urban ones, it is an exceptionally fast reforesting which takes place- such is the case in the modern age with the city of Detroit, in which about half of all residential areas are abandoned or, at most, host to squatters- the fact that beavers have begun to move back into an area which hadn't seen any in a century shows us the result of a lowered human population. In the post atomic world, though, many species will be under their own stress and population constraints due to disease.

There are many risks however in extracting materials from abandoned structures, ruined areas, and even from nature. There will be no tetanus vaccines in this post apocalyptic world, and something that we would currently not worry about- say, a small cut- could become infected easily. There will be broken glass, exposed steel, and probably half rotten meat and other organic matter littered everywhere. This is why sanitation must be undertaken quickly, to dispose of as much contaminant as possible; not just corpses, as I said, but detritus- literally any organic matter capable of decomposing.

It won't be possible, either, to maintenance buildings for the most part and without any maintenance, the rate at which they will begin to crumble will be far higher than currently. Poorly built structures will be the first to go- the way some buildings are made they function almost like a greenhouse, and if they have been flooded by destroyed pipe systems or sprinklers they will function quite literally in the same manner. There are already abandoned buildings whose lower levels have become little more than warm swamps, sometimes even containing fish, and all containing various insects and photosynthetic life forms, which will always move into areas which have been neglected.

Standing water should be destroyed when possible to cut down on the mosquito population. Many of their hosts will have died and their population will briefly collapse (due to this and then fallout) but will spike thereafter as their competitors die off as well, having been poisoned at a greater rate.

For those who wish to scavenge, their own personal health should be protected- protective clothing (anything from a leather trench-coat and leather gloves to a hazmat suit and kevlar) will prevent injury to some extent, and injuries can be treated topically. Without antibacterial substances widely available, isopropyl alcohol and sulfur will be in demand. The latter can be crushed and applied to a wound, most often preventing it from becoming infected. Topically, crushed white sage also contains antimicrobial substances. As for viruses, other than lowering fever there is little anyone will be able to do.

Here I can make a prediction which may or may not come true after such events; the release of heat around blast sites, coupled with fallout both from atomic war itself and the subsequent melting down of many nuclear plants, will combine to severely reduce the bacterial action of the world. This will temporarily dumb down the infection rate of most bacterial diseases (and may wipe some out entirely.) But will, down the road of time, lead to a far higher mutation rate thereof; as such, if medical systems are not re-established within a few decades, a whole host of new mutant strains of disease may take hold. Influenza, currently pandemic every year, will be less able to spread and infect fewer people when world trade dies down to a mere crawl- so there is a benefit and a detriment to the effects of radioactivity- remembering that radioactive beams are currently used to bombard some foodstuffs to sterilize them; this is largely effective (albeit controversial because people don't understand what gamma rays are.)

The reduction of bacterial action may be "good" for the sterilization of some infectious agents (including exotic diseases kept in storage in pharmaceutical and government labs- which is a terrible idea), but it will be quite bad for those undertaking agriculture- bacteria are necessary for proper crop growth, and as well bacteria within the human body help to keep the digestive tract especially, in a healthy state- chronic exposure to contamination will likely wrack the human population with digestive issues, although the contamination will be outlasted by the gut flora in question, and ultimately this may be seen as temporary.

This too will affect scavenging for materials. Food that would otherwise be digestible may end up causing some who eat it to be sickened inexplicably. If this happens, it may be the result of lack of (or changes to) digestive bacteria- and there won't be a lot of probiotics available (specifically, dairy products) because in mere days every bit of yogurt and milk will be curdled and spoiled, having largely gone unrefrigerated.

With the world shifting to vegetarianism due to lack of safe meat available, the carrying capacity of the world will actually increase once contamination dies down. Scavenging for seeds will be exceptionally important; however, only self-replicating, heirloom, non-GMO seeds should be planted. Only if starvation is looming should anything else be planted. Manipulative firms have rendered most of the world's crops sterile, but heirloom crops will be available. Decades after the war, when trade is partly restored, unique heirloom seeds will command a hefty premium, and of that you can be sure. Guard them as though they were made of gold.

In fact we should speak briefly *of* gold. Or rather, valuable metals and jewelry and similar things which may be stockpiled or lifted thereafter. We often hear the claim that gold and silver and other precious metals and gems have *intrinsic value.* That is, their value is not artificial, and they will always be in demand.

I question the usefulness of gold or silver in such a situation- it isn't self replicating or edible, and its primary use is in electronics and for industrial purposes; but this world is one with little of both for some time, and will be rather focused on obtaining safe food, water, and construction materials, after which the other rudiments of "normal" life follow. You may as well declare bottlecaps a form of currency. It does, however, make sense for groups to maintain some precious metals as a form of good which can be used once trade is restored. Bartering will have largely replaced actual currency because the making of currency (and issuing it to any form of agreement between groups) will be difficult.

If after the apocalypse I have a bag of couscous, and two hungry people show up and make offers in exchange for it, and one offers me a bar of gold and the other a bag of heirloom tomato seeds, I am likely to take the trade of the latter; not because gold is a bad thing, or lacks potential value, but because in this world it is objectively worth less from a survival standpoint, than the tomato seeds are. If a third person offers me a brick of brimstone and a fourth a gun and ammunition, *then* there may be difficulty determining which good I want I return, but the gold will be useless to me for anything other than staring at and chuckling.

In fact, precious metals are far more useful for less drastic situations; a recession, a depression, some sort of temporary disorder. Without food and water for survival, and weapons and shelter to defend your gold, the gold is useless, but if you have the former you may not even need the latter. So while grabbing gold and silver is a great idea for protecting your wealth in the case of economic problems, it may be more trouble than it's worth for other purposes. I have spoken with some survivalists and it sounds like gold is usually fairly low on the priorities list.

And when one considers the orderless, post-apocalyptic nuclear world with its craters and lack of law enforcement, one might say that a man with a gun and body armor can just *take* that gold, without permission, at any time. If this is the fear then the weapon is surely better than the gold. And if you're half starved and thirsty, a brick of gold won't buy you a drink and a meal unless someone is willing to denote it as valuable enough to justify expending precious resources in exchange.

This opinion will likely be unpopular with some who claim to be forward-thinking. I have spoken in times past with others and noted that precious materials are exceptionally good ideas for recessions and exceptionally bad ideas for all-out disorder. The more disorderly the situation, the less typically valuable objects and things are needed or desirable, and the more desirable becomes food, water, shelter, and the ability to defend oneself; it is a simple concept; the higher mental functions and thus higher functions of organized society break down in stages.

In the case where everything is normal, currency is desirable. It is used as a standard of exchange by all- we might even say electronic (imaginary) cash is higher than physical cash now for some purposes.

In the case where there has been disturbance without breakdown, wealth reverts to a lower stage; gold and silver being the highest amongst the substances here, but also gems, jewelry of other metals, platinum, and so forth.

In the case of a larger-scale breakdown, the ability to defend oneself is the most valuable. Water and food may still be available but driving down the road carries the possibility of being attacked. We might see this as similar to the LA riots or something of that nature. Observe that cash and precious metals did not defend the victims of this wave of violence, yet they did not run out of food or water.

For a complete breakdown, the ability to defend is peripheral and predominantly a safeguard for the real wealth sources; which are water, food, medically active substances, shelter, and above all *land itself* which is capable not of being eaten but actively generating food and water. Although it will be available to anyone willing to work it, land alone has the highest post-apocalyptic value.

Thus I say, scavenging trinkets of gold and silver may be fun (it would be interesting to see a whole box of gold and silver and diamonds, to be sure) but it may or may not lead to any form of stability. It also becomes a potential target for looters.

PRESERVING KNOWLEDGE IS PENULTIMATE

When I stated that land, food, water, and weapons were of the highest value in a truly post-cataclysmic world, I spoke primarily of physical, tangible things, with physical, tangible value.

However, there are two things perhaps more valuable than these; although their value is long-term rather than based on the concept of surviving and preventing further disorder and mortality than will have already occurred.

In reality, there is a potentially greater value to knowledge itself, and subsequent to this, the means of production- the capacity and resources necessary to continue producing machined or processed items. If food is important, the ability to preserve it is also such; and while some food resources can be stored for fairly long periods without protection by canning, pickling, and so forth, the ability to produce vinegar for pickling, the ability to mine or otherwise obtain salt, and things such as this will become increasingly important as well; it will be up to organized groups to obtain the means to do so. Here, we have knowledge required to do so, and the ability to create or maintain the machines or resources to do the same.

Even the ability to make alcohol will be important; both as a form of recreation (to reduce stress on the population) and as a potential medical aid- for anesthesia will be limited to getting the patient drunk or stoned, for some time. Opium poppies may be grown for the latter.

Imagine, for a moment, a population of individuals which has formed such a group. They may have a great deal of ammunition, but if they run out of the same will they be capable of creating nitroglycerin and machining bullets or will they revert to wielding bows and arrows? They have food, but can they store it such that it precludes starvation by preventing spoilage? They have, perhaps, access to water, but can they filter it? Can they drill a well or power it with solar cells or a generator?

These things will be increasingly important; the availability of pre-fabricated goods will decline over time as degradation sets in and the population recovers, with all working systems of the same nature eventually owned by individuals or groups. The re-establishment of communications will also be of the highest importance; especially shortwave radio systems. HAM radio systems for receiving signals are common, but broadcasting will require electricity and a working system; in rural areas, stumbling upon a location equipped to do so lowers the threshold of needed resources to two things; the electricity to make the shortwave work and the necessary knowledge to maintain it. For the purposes of this work, I will not explain it in depth but leave it instead to the reader to study it themselves from other works, which are numerous. Other forms of communication will be far more difficult to establish. Shortwave is relatively easier to maintain and power than telephone lines or something of that nature, as it makes use of the ionosphere and requires no cable maintenance. So long as the broadcasting center contains at least one person able to fix it should it break, it can provide communication and recreation; perhaps broadcasting music.

Musical knowledge may sound unimportant but it is not; first because it contains cultural treasure akin to anthropologically important (archaeological) remains at physical sites, and second because broadcasting such a signal provides a potential beacon to the larger outside world, as well as a recreation for any local populations, which can then listen to the same music. A computer hooked into such a system and continuously powered by solar cells and batteries will be able to ease the conditions of the surrounding population by providing a distraction from simply "surviving." As such, other computers should be requisitioned, in order to obtain more material to broadcast- a single USB drive can store many songs, and if randomized and played continuously would roughly mimic the track listings of any decent radio station, as such stations typically focus only on one or a few genres; but this shortwave station can play anything from classical compositions, to Gothic rock, to heavy metal, to all the hits of the pre-atomic world. Staving off boredom is of importance; there was a time in man's history when the colder months were mostly spent half drunk and huddled in bed because the means to travel and move about was limited and roads unsafe and poorly maintained- short of expending massive effort in alleviating such conditions this may loosely approximate the new world post-war at large.

Shortwave systems may even be able, depending on the facilities, to communicate with and broadcast to great distances- some signals are powerful enough to be heard all around the world, although the means to power such a long-distance broadcast will be difficult to obtain. A regional broadcast is more within reach.

It may of course be a good idea not to broadcast works which revolve around war- people will not likely take kindly to such things. There could indeed be multiple sites broadcasting different things- one station to serve as an informational, pre-recorded site where instructions on survival and also movement to and from various locations can be given, another for music, and so on.

Here I will submit a further theory- we are currently in an age where alternative energy is becoming more widespread and more efficient, especially in Europe and the United States. The longer this atomic war is prevented the better, from the standpoint of attempting to rebuild various societies after the exchange which is all too likely to occur; if society has largely become reliant on solar cells, windmills, and electric engineering for transportation by the time of the war, especially if these things become prevalent in rural areas less likely to be attacked and destroyed, the world will recover far more rapidly. If factories dedicated to creating such energy sources, paired with areas where the raw materials needed are found, are quickly populated, it should be possible for very little energy interruption to be experienced in those areas; this is fortunate, for it means the ability to machine goods, use vehicles, and maintain life will be less reduced overall. In such an area, life will be far more livable than in areas lacking such capabilities, but even if the means to maintain and create such windmills and solar cells do not exist, their ability to create power may outlive the unavailability of new systems comparable to the ones already installed.

The knowledge of how to build and maintain such energy and communications systems is secondary only to obtaining the means to craft them- thankfully, man had already developed shortwave systems in the 1920s and so the technology required to make and maintain them dates to an era when coal was the primary energy resource and vast areas of the world were still reliant on wood heating and had no electricity. Connecting settled, re-organized areas through such systems would be simple if alternative energy is associated with their use, and thus no additional extraction of resources was needed beyond factories used for manufacturing new solar cells or windmills.

Here is another proposition to the survivors; quickly craft your production of energy-supplying goods to use alternative energy to make yet more alternative energy. Think of a factory making solar cells, which in turn is powered by its own solar cells; as such, the cycle is self sustaining and the span of production ever increasing. It will require that those with knowledge regarding engineering commandeer such areas that they may, for such purposes.

Another important knowledge to retain is that of fighting fires. In the post apocalyptic world there may be a series of wildfires if areas have become withered by fallout- dry, dead forests and grasslands are vulnerable, and these fires may advance on populated settlements. A cleared expanse- a sort of no-man's land- around organized settlements will work for this purpose, although flooding the surroundings by diverting a stream may also be of use. Again, engineering knowledge will be needed to do so.

Here I will say; much of what we consider modern culture emerged around the early 1900s, about a century ago. This age of dirigibles and early skyscrapers and radio systems, marked by the electrification of urban centers, of flashing lights and automobiles, is where modernity begins. Only a few facets of postmodernism are truly required to perpetuate knowledge- predominantly computers- these will be difficult at first to manufacture, but they can be requisitioned and maintained in vast numbers if organized groups do so quite quickly. Establishing enough electricity to keep running a few computers ensures greater ease of access to educational materials which may be found on various detachable media; every CD or flash drive may have priceless digitized books or something similar on them. As for physical media, books and such, these are even more valuable (and won't eventually stop working due to age alone.)

Because so many trappings of civilization come from just the last few generations, we might think of the post-atomic world not as a throwback to the stone age but more a steampunk-style fusion of very old and rather new- even the severely decreased world population is likely to stabilize at several billion if people amalgamate and organize and repair the world to the best of their ability. Instead of a near human extinction, the world may after only a few decades be equivalent to what it was like in the middle of the 1900s with concerted effort. Keeping this in mind, a population persists and has a reason to strive to keep existing, otherwise it may lose hope, splinter, and fall into intellectual darkness.

YOU WILL PROBABLY GET CANCER

Now comes the time for a bit less fortunate news; in this highly radioactive world, the rate of cancer and other, similar problems will have risen drastically. Not all is bad, though- most individuals will still live to what we consider a decent age so long as they have survived early childhood- they will, rather, pass away due more to cancer than stroke and heart disease, as are prevalent in modernity.

Our current western culture suffers mortality largely due to excess rather than need; a century ago starvation was the biggest factor in premature mortality, but lately the bigger problem is obesity, lack of exercise, and poor diet- not poor in the sense of too little food, but rather poor in the sense of too much, or sometimes too high a proportion of nutrient-lacking foods which fill the diet with crap that is barely edible.

As such, one problem is traded for another in the post-war situation; humans will find themselves once again working harder to obtain food and water, and although as I said this will quite quickly be solved by organization, there will be a period in which famine, not overeating, will be the major issue involved in mortality. Rather than look at this as a "bad" thing we might even say it's about the same as our current situation. Humans naturally seek what is less available; in the ancient world, being a bit chubby was desirable and rich foods carried a premium. In modernity, in the developed world, being thin as a rail is considered beautiful and organic foods and raw foods more expensive than processed ones!

The replacement of the human ideal thus may take place; where once being slim was desirable, now in the world will having a bit of extra weight be seen as the ideal of beauty- not because such an ideal is objective (for it is artifice) but because of the difficulty in obtaining it. As always, man's psychology fixates upon and desires that which is less easily obtained; this even explains the fixation with gold and silver and other "precious" things which have a utilitarian purpose but not any more so than other, more common substances and objects.

Although you may indeed die of cancer, you must simply ask yourself if this is any more horrific than your high chance of suffering from a heart attack in the modern sense. The objective answer, of course, is "no." In either case, humans are mortal and the pain of dying of some disease is about the same; perhaps it will even be less suffering than before, as the population stops being hit by waves of obesity, diabetes, and heart problems.

There is a potential psychological benefit as well, strange as it may seem. So many people sit at desks for forty hours a week to get pieces of paper and a pat on the head. Now, though, the average human will not only spend a great deal of time in nature, but will have far less social constraint on their activities. A person will be able to dress as they wish, rather than wearing a uniform. They will be able to play around in abandoned buildings, so long as they accept the risk thereof. The nanny state mentality of many urban areas will be replaced with one of curiosity and adventure, for the world will have temporarily shrunk around them, leaving that which lies beyond their fence or wall as unknown space.

There is another thing to be mentioned here as well; the amount of radioactivity the survivor will be exposed to may not, depending on their area, even be as high as the amount a smoker is exposed to should they light up half a pack of cigarettes a day. Cigarettes are known to contain a fairly high amount of radioactivity, and that level isn't degrading with every pack they open. For the rest of the population, the radioactivity level will slowly go back down to background levels- a bit higher since some of that background is courtesy of man-made sources, specifically nuclear testing from the 1940s through the 1990s. In a century, the levels will be, in most areas, lower than they will be before the war itself, with the exception of areas in proximity to highly contaminated regions around nuclear plants which have been destroyed or destabilized and melted down. Such sites should be marked off and warnings placed there to ward anyone away from getting too close, and those with radiological gear can take initiative to do so.

So while your risk of cancer may rise, your risk of other maladies resulting from inactivity and overeating will be considerably lower. The life expectancy in areas which have restored electricity and industry will probably be similar to life expectancies we currently enjoy, because they will be privy to clean water, stable food intake, and sanitary conditions for medical care, after enough effort has been made to restore the same.

YOUR CHILDREN WILL LIKELY BE DEFORMED

The title of this section is deliberately exaggerated. The human body is capable of withstanding radioactivity at a great enough level so that most of the population will persist in general health, and those with mutations may have symptoms which are perfectly survivable- say, someone with a mild deformity of the fingers, or an extra set of toes. While morbid, I needed to include this section to prepare survivors for what may come.

As we see in the region around Chernobyl, populations exposed to radiation *do* suffer a higher rate of deformity. This has an effect on survival and health that is higher than what authorities admit to, and lower than what the general population believes. As such, it will not cause extinction, although it may make life difficult. You should be prepared to witness the occasional stillbirth or child with grievous deformity, as well as those who are "almost normal" but have, say, an odd feature about them, or two.

Human populations have survived several bottlenecks and subsequent inbreeding. They have also survived fallout before in zones at Chernobyl and Fukushima. They have survived various natural disasters ranging from super-volcanic explosions to asteroid impacts- drought and flood alike have never destroyed all humans, and almost never even all members of local populations regardless of the level of destruction caused. As such, human extinction is unlikely, following a nuclear war- human suffering, though, is certain.

I provide this section and its somewhat morbid content only to prepare the reader for the possibility of such suffering; but birth rates will necessarily rise and the genetic lineage will slowly repair itself through the selective survival of the fittest individuals, allowing them to overpower those who have become genetically unhealthy. I speak not of eugenics or a master race but nature's own ability to remove deleterious mutations over time. In fact, human beings alone have provided a safe haven for such mutations solely through their own medical knowledge; centuries ago many of the mutations in our own gene pools would never have persisted at any visible level through the dying off of unfit individuals, sad or psychologically cold as it may sound; for it is nature, not man, that reigned at the time.

Infant mortality will also be more prevalent, although because of modern medical knowledge being perpetuated (even if not all modern procedures and compounds will be available) the level will likely be lower than in man's fairly immediate past, say the early 1900s. A few generations will experience more stress than before, and during this period a baby boom is likely, and as modernity encroaches, the death rate will slacken once more. It is thus up to the survivors to reorganize and attempt to preemptively fix the problems with former society which caused such calamity to begin with; namely opaque government, warmongering, paranoia, and the advancement of weapon technology for no purpose other than delusion.

HOW TO OUTFLANK AND DESTROY ANY ENEMY REMNANT

Although it is likely that most survivors will have conglomerated themselves into largely defensive groups, there will also possibly be those that form militias for the sole purpose of establishing corrupt order all over again; rule by the few, or the dictator, or the military ruler-ship of the junta. These groups may also be paired with remnants of former rule- the wealthy with private bunkers and armies, or perhaps dishonest political figures (also sheltered in bunkers, with these areas paid for by taxes) in bed with various elites and corporate heads.

In any case, these folks are not likely to emerge for some time- the bunkers are well stocked for them, and it's possible some of them both knew the war was impending beforehand and at the same time abandoned the population to be destroyed or crippled; as such they must be considered enemy combatants, guilty of treason against their respective nations. It is possible some such groups will splinter and fall into disorder within their hidey-holes before they even get a chance to emerge, which is beneficial, because it reduces their forces should multiple such groups exist in tandem with one another for nefarious reasons.

Such bunkers are obviously outside the means of most to directly assault, but there are ways to destroy them nonetheless.

If such an area is found to be sealed and thus likely inhabited, and the bunker is thought to belong to some billionaire oligarchical plutocrat, or a military unit which intends to rise once more to install their corrupted order, the first option is to destroy the bunker by destroying its ventilation system- there will be vents, whereby air is drawn into the bunker, and although it will be heavily filtered (you couldn't just vent smoke into the bunker to asphyxiate them) it would be easy enough to seal the ventilation system so no air at all was entering the bunker. Then, it merely becomes a waiting game.

Such areas typically would have eyes on the outside- cameras and such. Blind the inhabitants by destroying these cameras or microphone systems. Prepare to dig in around the entrance (likely to be singular, or multiple entrances in the same general area.) It may make just as much sense to simply bury the entrance with debris if it is possible- often they are located on the sides of mountains, so explosives set above the entrance can be used to cause rock slides, blocking their exit altogether.

Because the firepower of such shadowy remnants is likely to be greater than outside groups even if they grab up gear from a military base or police station which has been abandoned, it is a bad idea to confront them directly. Rather, disable the ability of the bunker to function, forcing them out like ants as the rain floods their nest. Since they likely possess high explosives even a rock slide may just slow their exit down, but perhaps it is possible to penetrate the ventilation systems and damage the filters, also.

I speak here largely of private orders and figures, rather than the well established bunkers held by the US political system itself as well as other political groups across the world. While we may regard politicians as dishonest, it is unlikely their first thought upon exiting and seeing the ruined world will be about how to conquer it all. Rather, the real threat could emerge from some billionaire's bunker out in the mountains somewhere- the Mormons have an extensive mountain bunker system in Utah which they would probably evacuate their own leadership to if able. Additionally, I do not speak of smaller private bunkers which individuals or families have built- they should be left alone, and in fact aided if the possibility to communicate with them exists; such forward-thinking individuals would be invaluable, since they obviously possess grit and knowledge.

The next threat would come from the same looters already mentioned, as well as perhaps the occasional outlaw. When we regard a quasi-anarchic world our immediate thought is that in the lawless state crime would be rife; rather it's likely to be fairly rare, and where it exists would likely be limited to swiping food or medical supplies, since every would-be criminal would be faced with surroundings filled with other survivors which wield firearms or other weapons. It would be a dangerous world altogether but far more so for one who intends to survive by taking from others. Actual criminals are likely to have starved in their locked cells during the war, and so millions of rapists, murderers, thieves, and other figures will have been executed by nature.

There is a similarity here with the wild west; every movie and cartoon depicting the era depicts it as one of outlaws by the dozen with one or two "good guys" with six shooters and good eyes mowing them down in endless waves. This couldn't be further from the truth- lawlessness was typically *rare* in the wild west because almost everyone carried firearms with them. Crime was, in fact, far more prevalent in the *east* in the United States, where most individuals carried no weapon and only the police existed to protect the disarmed from bandits and thugs of various types.

Rather, in the case where order has mostly broken down, the main threat other than animals or ruins in poor repair collapsing on your head will be simple bandits in groups moving around trying to survive- they will as always attempt to remain hidden and not be discovered rather than confront what may be larger or better armed groups directly- because criminals operate on the principal of risk and reward. If the pay-off is not worth the risk, the action is less likely to be undertaken unless the person is psychotic.

These groups are unlikely to exist in large numbers, because of the availability of free land and free goods. The likelihood is higher of roving groups of scavengers who slowly become marginalized and shun society due to their observation of its former collapse. These groups will likely not be a threat to more organized groups which have re-settled areas.

SANITATION AND DISEASE REDUCTION

I have spoken already of the need to remove detritus and attempt to decontaminate areas, however there are further ways to specifically reduce disease in re-settled areas.

In some parts of the world, ticks are quite common; and they're also exceptionally tough- it's not certain that fallout will substantially reduce their numbers, when feral hosts will multiply rapidly. Long grass and brush harbors these feigns, as they climb up branches and blades and simply wait with outstretched legs, until some unfortunate animal waddles by, after which they climb right on board for a snack of blood. Most ticks carry little disease, but Lyme disease especially would probably be a death sentence in the post-atomic world, as treatments will not be available. Upon finishing any form of outdoor work in an area known to harbor tick populations, the survivor ought to check their body- including their clothes because at times they hitch a ride indoors on a pair of pants and then climb off to find a host. Destroy them wherever you find them. Trimming grass will help reduce their prevalence around dwelling places- a lawn mower usually requires fuel, but manual push-mowers do exist and they're not as difficult to use as some seem to believe, so long as the grass is not allowed to become too deep at any time so that the blades can keep it trimmed to a decent length.

Fleas are another bane of society; there was a time years ago when fleas were extremely uncommon in my area owing to cold weather, but we had a major infestation of them one year, when the winter was extremely mild, and both animal and man were covered in them. Thankfully, nobody became diseased, but a flea population in the post atomic world may carry plague among other things, as rodents spill forth from damaged sewers and migrate around intermixing with potentially rural but infected populations.

Unlike ticks, which only thrive in areas with long grass (for ants and other insects will eat them if they cannot obtain such an area, sometimes) fleas will exist anywhere. Rodents should be trapped, poisoned, or otherwise destroyed as effectively as possible. Mouse traps will be widely available, as will rat poison- as for other small mammals, it is not generally even necessary to bait a trap. One year, my garden was being invaded by various creatures- skunks, moles, and a groundhog. I killed every single one of them by simply finding where they were coming in and trapping them. I destroyed the groundhog, five skunks, and about a dozen moles (which had nested under the compost pile. When I found this out, I ripped it open and destroyed the nesting members.) There was a time at which I hurled a pitchfork at one mole, which had returned to find its nest gone- it speared it through the head and killed it instantly. This may seem grotesque but it will be necessary in the post apocalyptic wasteland for anyone who wishes to survive very long. Care should be taken not to harm any small carnivores such as cats. They should be given flea collars if possible.

Standing water breeds mosquitoes. In the modern age a great many formerly swampy areas have been drained but the drainage systems will begin to degrade and fail over time and some of these former swamps will revert back to wetland status. There is a plant called lemon balm which when rubbed on the skin smells like citron and repels mosquitoes, along with black flies, although deer flies seem not to care. Mosquitoes kill more humans than anything else through their diseases, although mostly the tropical regions are host to the sub-species carrying, say, malaria.

The best treatment for any insect-borne illness is to prevent transmission in the first place. Repellants and citronella candles will be available for some time, but these will run out eventually, and other measures will need to be taken. Wearing long clothing, and stuffing the bottom of the pants into your socks, will provide excellent coverage, with any exposed skin treated with lemon balm or some other plant to repel the horde.

Any diseased animal, when encountered, should be killed unless the nature of the disease is known outright not to be communicable (as in, the semi-domesticated rodent killing cat is just sick because it ate too much grass.) The corpse should be burned where it falls, using kerosine or wood, or any other flammable material nearby, so that it becomes sterile ash. Some individuals will not be able to bring themselves to euthanize animals, especially "cute" ones, so others will have to dedicate more time to this. As for the "ugly" species most people would probably kill them anyways.

There is also the threat of contamination in crops- not radioactivity, but rather contamination by fungus and pests- there is little that can be done, since pesticides will not be available, to cut down a horde of locusts (although they can be netted, roasted, and eaten for protein, and that's no lie- if seasoned they even taste fairly good.) Crops grown in boggy or poorly drained areas will be susceptible; especially to ergot in certain grains. Although corn requires far more nitrogen than other grains, it will not be infected with ergot, which can destroy a whole harvest if the infected kernels of rye or sorghum are stored along with good grain, if it is ground up together for use. Flint corn prepared with a weak lye from wood ash can be turned into a nutrient rich *hominy* and dried and stored for longer periods than sweet corn, although the lye-leeched corn must be then washed to remove any lye. Sweetcorn is *useless* as a nutrition source; stick with flint corn and leech it with wood ash; pour water through the ash and a screen, and collect the drained water to use for this purpose, soaking the kernels of flint corn. Do not touch the lye.

Wheat is somewhat safer than sorghum or rye- sorghum is especially susceptible it seems, for that which I myself grew was infected with ergot and my garden is not poorly drained. A double-legume setup may work well; grow the corn along with a nitrogen fixing crop (lentils, peas, string beans) and the following year just grow the legume again and not the corn, rotating the corn's location between two fields each year, so that there is always as much nitrogen being injected as removed. Make sure to compost plant remains and apply this to smaller beds for herbs or greens. Do not waste urine. Add it to charcoal and powder it and add this to the beds too to restore the soil.

If the soil is carbonized, properly grown, and not poorly drained it will be more resistant. A lot of the plague-like infestations of caterpillars, locusts, and other pests in the modern age only occur because the availability of grain crops for them to munch on is so high- hundreds of miles of mostly uninterrupted farmland exist in many parts of the world and as such the crops have to be frequently sprayed with dangerous chemicals. In the post-fallout world, the radiation will have killed some pests, and others will starve in the absence of agriculture. As such, if such an infestation occurs, it is best to manually destroy them with your bare hands if able; for locusts and grasshoppers, catch them and eat them. You can construct a sort of cooking utensil for this made with fine mesh screen shaped into a box with a handle. Put the locusts in there and hold them over a fire, shaking some salt and garlic or other herbaceous flavoring onto them. When they brown flip it over and do so to the other side. I have eaten raw and seasoned insects; raw, they are at best edible but not very flavorful. Seasoned, they are crunchy and delicious and satisfying. Those who find the idea repugnant may come around when they realize they will starve if they don't get their recommended two servings a day of protein-packed, slightly radioactive locusts. Cockroaches can also be eaten although they're a bit more disease prone. Ants can be eaten; in fact other than spiders and caterpillars most insects are perfectly edible; including grubs, which nonetheless are disgusting to anyone.

In this way the crops will be unimpeded by pests; pest damage can invite further disease into your fields.

I previously also spoke about how maintaining chickens (or other fowl) would be far more efficient and easy than maintaining pigs, cows, and other larger species for meat or, in the case of chickens, for eggs. This has the additional benefit of pest removal if they're free range and able to access your garden area (keeping them away from grains and other species of plant they may predate upon.) However, some types of disease do come from avian species. The chickens should not be allowed to live in squalor, caked in their own filth, but should be well fed, well housed, and their housing kept as clean as possible.

The benefits of these animals; as a food source and for pest removal, as well as their inability to be infected with rabies, far outweighs the possibility that they will spread some avian diseases. Some medication for them may be available; I am unsure of its shelf life, and mortality will exist for some chickens which will have been poisoned by radioactivity. Keeping them fed and predator free, as well as clean, will allow them to be reproduced infinitely; in fact you might prepare for some mortality as the result of having to cull members once everyone has a stable, reproducing population, specifically because they will out-breed their surroundings. Allowing them to pack themselves in by the thousands *will* bring disease because they will begin to starve for resources- even though you will likely be feeding them certain grains yourself to augment their free range dietary content. Free range is better than caged, for a large proportion of their food will thus not be your responsibility, as they peck down caterpillars and grubs in your garden.

BASTARDIZED LEGALISM LEADS TO DESTRUCTION: HOW WE HAVE ERRED

In truth nuclear war would perhaps not be so likely as it currently is were we to immediately do away with a great deal of bad government and legalism in the world; this is the case regardless of the culture. It may sound like a bit of a corny reference, but nuclear weapons are a bit like the ring of power from Tolkein's lore; an object of enormous power that nonetheless can only be used to destroy, corrupt, and warp- such is the way of such a weapon which is mostly indiscriminate and would necessarily cause mass casualties among civilian populations.

When the atomic bombs first created by the United States were deployed, they were not used against military targets; the only purpose to using them at all on largely defeated Japan was to psychologically shock them into absolute submission, convinced that their entire culture would be wiped out if they did not capitulate fully. Rather than use such weapons on bases away from civilian regions, they were dropped on Hiroshima and Nagasaki, killing over 100,000 people in just two explosions. The firebombing of Dresden as elsewhere proved that the allied forces were already capable of leveling cities with conventional weapons, but for the psychological goals of Truman and others, only the most terrifying weapon would suffice, and it was not enough to simply undergo scorched earth policy towards Japan- after all, the Japanese navy and air force had already been decimated and they did not have the ability to repulse even a conventional bombing campaign.

Generally there, as elsewhere, state propaganda (which was used by all sides, not just the losing side which western culture typically regards as "the bad guys") enforced the view that the foe was subhuman, or simply evil; as such the populations' consciousness regarding the use of such a horrifying power was substantially reduced. We never would have had an arms race at all, had the people of the United States and former USSR not been pumped day and night full of "patriotic" rhetoric and constant denigration towards the other "side." Really, the civilians themselves would have rather seen themselves as fellow humans, equally doomed should the arms race continue, and likely would have demanded an end to hostility. This actually happened during the late 1960s and early 1970s with mass protests, although in that case most grievance was against destroying villages in Southeast Asia across Vietnam, Laos, and Cambodia, and had little to do with atomic weapons, which were already at that time fully developed and available in large numbers to the USA and USSR.

In all cases, the development of such systems would not have been undertaken beyond the stage of energy development (if at all) were the cultures involved not run by idiots who felt compelled by egotism to make them. In order to get the population to support the creation of weapons only useful for destroying civilians and agricultural land, it was first necessary to make use of enormous amounts of propaganda, coupled with everything else we see as standard cold war intrusion; espionage, censorship, secrecy, and militarism on a mass, industrialized scale. A killing machine, essentially.

If the population of the USA or USSR knew that the sole purpose of such systems was specifically to eventually use them against an artificially crafted eternal foe, to destroy all human life within such a region, they likely would not have supported such a thing; but the propaganda convinced them that the other side would develop nuclear armaments on a massive level regardless. Thus, both nations framed their own programs in terms of defense, not offensive usage- as such the population mostly fell in line.

This has had the effect of a self fulfilling prophecy in the same way the so-called war on terror has had; the paranoia of the population rose quickly in the wake of spending several decades constantly reminded that death was fifteen minutes away and that everything they held dear could suddenly be crushed and immolated by missiles fired from the other side of the world; the same governments that for so long managed to pacify the population by reminding them the other side was the aggressor, in turn got engulfed by the "we're all going to die so let's party" mentality, as well as various pacifistic or armageddon-worshiping cults and social movements. Social Marxism, so long feared in the west, has now become more prevalent specifically *because* people have come to realize how bad their own so-called representation is. Nationalism, so long feared in the east, has now become more prevalent for the same reason.

In fact, the legalism and militarism of the cold war which perpetuated such weapons programs unwittingly laid the groundwork for their eventual use and the annihilation of humanity; perhaps some intended it to be so.

LIVING IN PEACE WITH PEACEABLE FOREIGNERS

After the ashes, it is likely that any organized group will occasionally encounter those of foreign nationality, language, race, or culture, which naturally will have migrated around seeking areas they imagine to be more hospitable than those they originally inhabited. In the vacuum created by the war, in which land will be freely available, there is no specific reason to worry about such a thing; rather, any survivor which is peaceable should be welcomed after proper caution has been taken.

Let us now remember; the Western world became settled and powerful specifically because it began to absorb people from around the world; Rome had the same advantage and, like the rise of the dark ages, its eventual collapse came not because of its embracing of foreign religions or languages, and instead was brought about by their eventual abandonment of tolerance (within their laws and accepted practices, at least) towards such other foreign groups. Rome's problems began around the same time that they became more insular and built walls instead of expanding, and around the time they began weakening themselves by resorting to mercenaries such as Alaric, who would later attack and sack Rome itself specifically because his starving mass of soldiers had been mistreated (he felt) by the same Romans who had been paying him to attack other enemies of the same.

The best culture is one in which outsiders are welcomed and presumed to be peaceable until they show themselves to be otherwise, in which the limitation upon this acceptance is the willingness or lack thereof of the outside culture to adopt the basic rudiments of the super-culture they have enjoined. The two alternatives are the culture which is too tolerant and sees itself destroyed because it fails to recognize the difference between assimilating outside groups, and those seeking to usurp (such is the case in modern day Sweden) or the insular culture which spurns outsiders or mistreats them (such is the case in modern day Russia.) In both of the latter cases the culture suffers, whereas the open but lawful culture will generally persevere. The United States has had the same problem recently, whereby the native population appears in part to be incapable of differentiating between immigrants who wish to *become* American and those who are here for other purposes; as such the left has migrated towards a Swedish style way of thinking and the right has migrated towards that of Russia; the former embraces all foreigners without caring to make sure there is actual assimilation occurring (and some of the more severe leftists even shun the idea of assimilation and hate their own culture.) Likewise the right wing opposes all foreigners and appears to wish the nation was entirely walled off, which would ensure its death as it is out competed by more tolerant nations.

The future world power will be open but will expect those who join it to play by the same rules as everyone else.

Likewise, such a nation will need other facets to truly exist and thrive long term. It must be a culture into which the concept of individuality and freedom is deeply engrained. It must enshrine liberty, and strip its eventual organized governing body of much of the power current governments use, and must craft such stringent beliefs in such a way that they cannot be usurped.

However it must also be a patriotic culture; patriotism should be based solely around the idea of the culture as free, and the notion of skepticism towards all government and all government proposals will be a necessity, as well as an expansive right to self defense and self determination, otherwise the culture will end up as the modern United States has in which bastardized versions of "patriotism" are passed off as the real thing- namely unquestioning obeisance of government, or the idea that rights come from the government rather than a deity or natural law or sovereign recognition of the citizen's own inherent intellectual capacity to realize they are free.

A culture lacking such facets will be composed of a ruler or rulers and various subjects expected to show loyalty to the same. A culture possessing such institutionalized beliefs and defending them will be composed of a representative body and citizens which interchange with the same body freely. Such a culture must necessarily arise, and I have no worries that it will so long as initiative is taken by the survivors of the coming war; liberty and freedom are innate desires and despotism should always be met with hostility.

Intolerance shown to foreigners who have done nothing wrong will necessarily lead to hostility and, perhaps in time, to open aggression; in such a case it matters very little who is "right" or "wrong" because some will be killed on both "sides." Even the very idea of having sides, after there has been an atomic war, is rather laughable; the human race will be recovering from catastrophe and dedicating any great level of effort to destroying already crippled populations would be a monumental failure and show only that mankind deserved to be destroyed entirely, as a parasitic and horrific monstrosity, rather than a core of humanity being preserved and surviving the war itself.

Nor should moral laws even be considered; only when individuals are seen as individuals rather than members of some (usually meaningless) category will mankind recover in the first place; it was upon this founding basis that the very notion of revolutionary era liberty existed to begin with. A great deal of the morality that people have adopted is itself a corruption of liberty- the enshrining of hate and hostility, or the adoption of legalism which has the sole purpose of expanding the power of the few over the rights of the many and of the individual. It is for this purpose that all those alive today should be horrified to even consider the possibility that slavery or some similar system could continue and persist after such a war; the abolition of all totalitarianism by all surviving cultures ought to be a high priority, and people should live in freedom; liberty brings its own challenges but they are far fewer than those spawned when a small segment of the population has adopted its own power over others to the others' detriment.

After such an atomic war, the natural reaction to encountering others who are not of the same general culture, will be fear; fear of invasion perhaps, or displacement. It is highly unlikely that this will actually occur, because most advanced nations will have degraded as much as every other; an American, therefore, surviving the war, is more likely to encounter a Mexican or a Canadian than a column of Russian tanks advancing for the purpose of annexing what will be smouldering, radioactive wasteland. Nor is a Russian likely to encounter a column of American tanks, but is more likely to be visited by a Kazakh or someone from Finland.

Sadly, it is entirely possible that some cultures will be altogether exterminated in such a war; which ones will be subjected to this ultimate betrayal of reason is anyone's guess- smaller, more isolated tribes and subclasses of humanity are more fragile, and may be unable to cope with the cutting off of the world economy coupled with the fallout- it is also likely that secondary illness will decimate third world populations, especially in parts of Asia and Africa, while first world populations will be decimated by the war itself and a higher degree of radioactive contamination. It behooves even those well outside of any impact zones to prepare for the possibility of a breakdown in the world economy, because even desperately impoverished areas derive some degree of trade and technology from this trade system. For some years, it is unlikely that anything larger than a sailboat will be on the oceans, and it is unlikely that *anything* will be floating in open seas.

THE DANGER OF PARANOID ISOLATIONISM

There are much more severe and immediate dangers involved with isolation as well.

The first danger is biological; what will happen to the genetic lineage of a group which chooses to barricade itself into one area, and interbreed? The first generation or two will be fine; after all, inbreeding will not have had time to damage the genetics of the already radioactivity-soaked population. However, after a few generations, offspring will find it difficult to find a mate that isn't related to them-.

Inbreeding itself is not a problem if one of two things is true; either the population explodes in size and disperses before it becomes too prevalent, or the population is genetically healthy (as in, contains few or no deleterious recessive traits to begin with.) However, this post-atomic population's genetics have almost surely had some damage done to them, and the offspring may have mutations anyways. Inbreeding will naturally perpetuate such things, and it will fall into poor overall health.

The second problem of isolation is technological backwardness; the population, keeping to itself, is not necessarily privy to advances in energy or agricultural modes that have arisen elsewhere. Ten groups connected by trade and travel can interchange their advances and diversify labor in a manner that a single isolated group cannot. This group, in time, would eventually begin to resemble the Amish amongst us currently and would fall ever further behind.

The third problem is behavioral. A population which has isolated itself for any length of time will perhaps become even more isolated later; fearing or despising outsiders and adopting fanatic, cultist ways. I will give a warning about cults later in this guide, but the behavioral issue itself here due to isolationism is quite simple; the population is under stress and will be genetically weakened, and it may not be able to handle prolonged isolation on a psychological level. It may become so fearful of outsiders that it fortifies itself, locking the doors and bolting the windows- but what they themselves may imagine are defensive fortifications are really prison walls and they are the ones in a prison.

The fourth problem is that of resources. A smaller, more isolated group is more prone to die out due to famine or pestilence, where larger groups which connect with one another may be able to "shop around" for a solution to such problems. It would be odd indeed for a small neighborhood of mostly homogenous individuals to survive a nuclear war only to become as paranoid as our governments have been in modernity, emulating the same behaviors that doomed the world; and the group may well doom itself, because of the challenges involved in isolation.

There is then also the problem of social breakdown. The youth, especially, is prone to curiosity and rebellion. What then happens, should a horde of teenagers storm the wall and break through, leaving the nucleus of the population to wither as an entire generation abandons them for the outside? This may seem unthinkable, but it is surely possible in the absence of severe authoritarianism, which might be seen as the sixth possible problem.

THE DANGER OF UNCONTROLLED
COSMOPOLITANISM

While isolationism carries a severe penalty in any recovering population, its antithesis; that of virtually uncontrolled, laissez-faire cosmopolitanism also contains an element of danger. I submit that under some conditions such a near-anarchic system can work, has worked, and is even an improvement over rudimentary control for some purposes, but it requires balance nonetheless to be tenable.

A system in which there is no self preservationist element, and in which the members freely mix with others without regard to any form of social norms, will find itself subsumed in time by less tolerant movements; such has always been the case, as there will always be those who threaten with fire and sword. Totalitarianism, theocracy, and radical fanaticism seek such groups out and enslave them to their own views by taking advantage of hardship suffered by the more open and tolerant society, seizing power by convincing either the people as a whole, or those most heavily armed and physically fit, that they have the means to solve the problem. If they fail, they are ousted, and the problem may solve itself, but a charismatic movement of militaristic authoritarians can take hold in even the most cosmopolitan society, one with few to no moral components and no strictures or lawful basis, far more easily than they can overrun one which has created a libertarian but definitive basis upon which to operate.

The social order which has enshrined its own rights on paper and perpetuated them as part of a nation-state, and which has learned from the crimes and follies of the past, and which values its liberty above all else and actively prevents the rise of authoritarianism (just as it would the rise of isolationism) will be more likely to persevere than either the completely enclosed or completely open society.

The cosmopolitan's fate in fact is only positive if a larger, more powerful, more lawful society has taken it under its wing as an ally to protect them and to intervene should totalitarian or criminal elements emerge; this imbalance itself leads to problems as the larger culture necessarily pursues military means to secure its own fate and that of its smaller neighbor; this situation should be strenuously avoided.

The cosmopolitan also suffers another problem; in such a state where there is no control at all, a pestilence can spread with ease, because there is no means by which the population can prevent its members from encountering contagion. War can also erupt with ease, because there is no stricture against its members becoming militaristic and pursuing endeavors related to conquest or looting; the central culture may be averse to such things, but it will be judged along with the more warlike of its members if the culprits are identified and can be linked to the rest of the population. It is a dangerous system, almost as bad as isolationism, although it will prosper for a time as it openly adapts outside advances and very likely attracts immigrants.

THE WORLD WILL HEAL IF THERE IS ANYONE LEFT TO READ THIS

Take heart, though, reader; if the war has come and passed and anyone exists to read these words, then it means the world has not been killed off entirely. Many copies of this work may have been immolated already, but you, the reader, have survived, as has this copy of this work.

All things must pass; radioactivity does not last forever, nor will the charred remains of hundreds of cities always be in ruins. In time, nature will reclaim the ruins and they will become grasslands and forests; the world has regressed to an infant state, with some of mankind knocked back along with it- in the absence of large human populations, the trees will come back. If you look up at the night sky, you will likely see it is more colorful than before, with thousands and thousands of stars. If you had previously lived in a city you have probably never witnessed this before; even in my own small-town home the sky suffers from some level of light pollution despite being one of the more remote areas in the United States.

Most of man's laws will have passed away. There is nothing to stop you from scavenging alcohol or tobacco and using it. There is no longer a prohibition on your movement; no longer a highway you can't walk across because of automobiles, no longer a risk of being arrested for jaywalking. In a way, regardless of how broken and ill the world may look to you right now, it is arguably better in some ways than before.

It could be that I am still alive too as you read this, although it is hardly certain; I live far from any likely nuclear targets, but as I said, most nuclear systems do not have pinpoint accuracy and I am tolerably close to Boston, Massachusetts and Albany, New York- both are large cities. If I am alive I am probably doing just about what I was before I wrote this unless I have succumbed to fallout or frozen to death.

The likelihood stands, that some of the diseases endemic to man will have been excoriated from the world entirely by the decline in the human population plus the fallout- radioactivity will reduce biological content in most areas. Hemorrhagic fevers may be a thing of the past as well, and a good thing too because no treatment would exist for them after the ashes. Influenza, too, may finally decline in prevalence as poultry in Asia (where it spawns every year) is also decimated.

In the first few years after the war, nature will make slow progress reclaiming the ruins and the wastes- the lingering radioactivity will weaken the plants and make them susceptible to withering, but in time as the rains wash over the land, and as winter and summer slowly work the land, nature will recover the same as mankind will, and most humans will probably live in small pockets of population surrounded by what to them will seem to be infinite resources. This is an illusion- the world is smaller than we think. I have traveled a great distance in my life and you would be surprised how quickly you can move from the marginally temperate zones of New England to the steppe and heat of southern Texas.

If these populations have made use of renewable energy we might hope for a slightly utopian future of city states operating in tandem through trade and powering themselves with the sun, homes surrounded by step-gardens, populations connected once again through information technology; at first shortwave systems, and later on probably the internet will return as well. These self sustaining populations dotting the landscape, connected perhaps by paths, or by roads or trains, would be healthy, and surrounded by farms and further out the endless wall of forest. After the ashes, come the forests, and perhaps in a century someone will write a work by that title.

It could also be that the world will fall into barbarism and become dystopian. Perhaps remnant armies will come from their bunkers and establish a strict, corrupt state, or attempt to do so (and let us hope this is not the case.) It could be that mankind will fall into a new dark age; but mankind's collectively higher aptitude and literacy can be used to prevent this, for intellectual darkness was the cause and every other form the symptom, in those dark days of the medieval era.

The reader hopefully will dedicate themselves towards preventing this from happening- those who seek only to enslave and live the high life off of others' work must be stopped. For centuries they have endeavored to do just that, and just now as they have more wealth and power than ever, the world is worried that it will be destroyed by a sudden nuclear war, so we see the effects of their egotism and madness already, even before the warheads have exploded.

Catastrophism has become more and more common in the recent days of man- at least for a decade or so- people in the world are practically waiting for the bombs to drop, or a comet to streak out of the sky and cripple the world, or for a super-volcano to go off- there are many ways the world could be devastated by natural events alone, let alone due to mans' own efforts; this near-desire to see the world burn has arisen as a natural reaction to what is seen as an increasingly corrupted world in which there is a decreasing level of hope and decreasing upwards mobility for the lower classes, coupled with the general stagnation of spirituality as it begins to die off because its lies are exposed time and time again. People have abandoned what had been seen as mainstream principles for what may be seen as almost a cultist fanaticism revolving around materialism as well as a worship for death and chaos.

The citizens can hardly be blamed for this, because their so-called representatives and those with money and power in general have engineered the world in all its artificiality, leaving behind a vacuum in the average persons' psyche which they then seek to fill- it isn't their fault that they fill it with hate or violence, per se, because little else has been made available for them to absorb. Most people thrive in this artificial world where cheap manufactured crap with no purpose fills their early childhood, and cheap electronic crap fills their young adulthood. Cheap crap continues to fill their lives until they grow very old and realize they spent most of their life working to achieve exactly nothing at all, but by then they're too old to even become enraged enough to strike back at a system which had pumped them so full of trash.

At the same time, those that claim to care about the health of the earth- specifically the upper classes and elites pushing their environmentalist agendas, have apparently ignored the fact that their own private jets and mansions abuse the world far more than any hundred middle class citizens put together. This blatant hypocrisy is overlooked by the population at large because they seek out some sort of leader to change the world for them because they feel powerless to do so themselves.

As such, we can almost argue that the world can only be healed by catastrophe; the level of sheer corruption, waste, brutality, abuse, and evil that it contains is so great that it almost approaches spiritual proportions. While I am not a Christian and do not thus believe in Satan, all of their lurid tales about Satan might be easily and equally applied to some human beings and the comparison would be rather fitting.

It took thousands of years of hostility and vice to cripple and stagnate the world- if the same tendencies creep in after such a war, or any other apocalyptic event, the same will happen all over again. Perhaps man is trapped in such a cycle, by which every time he has a chance to regrow and renew, he fails and instead seeks out the same old familiar and corrupt order that existed before. It is my hope that man is not doomed to this fate and that whatever future incarnation of civilization arises will be better than the one that exists currently.

A WORLD WITHOUT BORDERS: THE GOOD, THE BAD, AND THE UGLY

In the coming world borders will in essence be a thing of the past- maintaining anything more sophisticated than a split rail fence or barricades made of scrap will be difficult for survivors at first, and even some time later anything beyond a cobblestone wall or perhaps barrier of cement slab will be beyond the means of most of the communities which will crop up.

It is likely that the advancement of culture insofar as civilization is concerned will follow a similar system to what happened in humanity's past, albeit on an accelerated time line. Thousands of years passed between the organization of the first rudimentary but organized village to the first city states, and from the city state to the kingdom, additional centuries passed. These lands, marked by collectives of individual city states which conglomerated together (in a manner similar to how we may regard the Deleon League of Greece) then gave way to cultural empires such as Rome in which there was a standardization across the entire controlled region. The modern nation comes later, although there are similarities.

It will not take thousands of years for man to return to modernity, but rather at most perhaps a few decades, because all the knowledge he has collected for thousands of years will still be available and, to some extent, already in the minds of survivors, who may be more fit than the general population was prior to the catastrophe.

This borderless world, however briefly it may exist, has its own problems and advantages.

One key advantage is simply that the transit routes made in times past can be corrected in accordance with new technology and mapping; often we see bizarre road systems which criss-cross over mountains rather than going under them in some way, because they were made before modern techniques were employed in building roads. Additionally, in the world as it will stand, it will probably make more sense to maintain smaller roads for bicycles and foot traffic, reserving larger cleared areas for mass transit such as train systems, which with existing technology can be made not only efficient but cheap to use- a train entirely plated with solar cells is capable of recharging itself between uses and hauling people or goods at little cost of fuel input.

It has additional advantages- the world of no borders allows people who formerly lived in relative slavery (incapable of movement without severe restriction) to move freely; while it may seem strange, it is altogether quite likely that those who lived under the most brutal regimes will become the most loving of this new freedom, because they understand the problems spawned by overt government or religious control. The world of no borders is also a world of absolute free trade. If the will exists to produce and move the products, the means are there to use those same skills at production to serve ones' own best interest.

There are however disadvantages as well. A world without borders is a world without defenses; and while open war is probably not likely in a realm where most or all standing armies are gone or severely weakened (and in which air and naval power are virtually nonexistent) the problem of petty crime- looting and arson and so forth- continues.

A world without borders will also be a difficult transition for those used to a world *with* borders. Simmering disputes over former borders are long lasting grudges and will not easily be forgotten, even after the administration of the same borders and disputes thereof have been ripped apart. We might expect that survivors in these zones will also be psychologically impacted, as they await with bated breath the possibility that some force from either claimant might march on them. The probability of this is very low- there will be so much fallow land that even establishing actual borders is hardly necessary in the short term, although possession is nine tenths of the law, and individuals as well as collective groups of individuals may lay claim to some tracts of land for the purposes of agriculture. We might say that even for the fairly long term it would be far more effective for groups to administrate small settlements, allowing the land between the same to remain fallow if possible so that nature too can recover- these areas will see their soil restored and their water systems slowly filtered of contamination over time, so that when the human population is ready to expand it will do so into a natural realm and not an artificial one filled with ruins, which will have begun to degrade swiftly.

The movement of people in and out of various areas should remain unimpeded. Here there are two types of impeding which may take place, both resulting from paranoia and/or legalism.

The first is that a culture may disallow all or some newcomers to join their ranks. At the very least if they intend to do so they ought to encourage trade and not abuse those simply moving through an area, since it will require multiple such settlements working in tandem to maintain even foot paths between them, and will require all that much more effort to maintain a wider throughway for bicycles or perhaps the occasional automobile or equestrian.

The second is more insidious and has already been discussed; the notion that a culture may fall into authoritarianism and bar its own members from travel, trade, or even movement altogether. Such despots should be overthrown. This includes, also, those who would falsely claim some level of power derived from titles that have been exterminated; there will be no sitting political authority which has attained its status through a proper vote or through documented monarchic succession, because all or most such members will have died, and those that have not may very well have even been complicit either in the war itself, or ignoring some other cataclysm, or in general corruption. It defies sense that they can adequately claim the right of leadership- either temporary or permanent- since they themselves may have been the agent of the nations' own demise. Nations, as we know them, will have to redevelop once the population has stabilized.

Those having resided in a former nation; say the United States, or Ireland, or China, or anything of that nature, may indeed consider themselves bound to that same national title, but they also need to remember that those living in areas formerly controlled by those now-decimated nations may be settled by those who want no part in such a national title. As such, these individuals, having picked their spot to settle in, assuming they are not waging war or perturbing others unduly, should be left alone.

Here is a diplomatic point for this borderless world; it is far more effective (as a means of preventing hostility) to encourage movement and trade and partnership, than it is to prevent it by going to war or remaining intellectually opposed to doing business with others. In the past we have seen many wars arise over mediocre differences of opinion, or from religious bickering, or fighting over resources which could instead have been traded freely; but we have *not* often seen wars waged between trading partners which have worked together to improve one anthers' infrastructure and capability of trade.

In the years after any worldwide catastrophe, the world will be marked as well by a return to nautical travel; the ocean is easier to travel across than land for any great length of trade, and indeed many areas are separated by ocean. Shortwave development will allow nations separated by the oceans to communicate prior to trade and travel, in order to coordinate it effectively and make such acts safer and faster.

FOUR OF CLUBS: IDENTIFYING FRIENDLIES

In the post apocalyptic world there is always the potential that identifying friend and foe will be difficult. It makes sense to provide some sort of system by which individuals can be identified at a distance, for the purposes of differentiating those of a particular culture from others. In ancient times, various insignia were used, especially for those who often wore armor which obscured the face- various symbolism also developed such as the tipping of the hat, which is rooted in the ancient use of full facial armor- a pair of soldiers thus lifted their visors to expose their identify- the handshake is the same and revealed that the person was not holding a weapon in what was generally their fighting arm (the right arm that is.)

There has already been talk amongst some in the online world that the four of clubs or a four leaf clover should be used by those specifically who are part of the culture of 4chan- an image board website with anonymous posting. This is a rather good idea; those who have built social webs on the internet more than in "real life" may actually find more camaraderie among those they have met there than with their own next door neighbors; although this does not necessarily mean the person's true identity is known to the other, it gives them something which binds them together, allowing them to interact in a somewhat informed manner.

We might here presume the use of two general insignia to be worn; something identifying former nationality (the colors or flag or some symbol of the nation once considered home) and any other secondary insignia showing that the person has been part of another group; perhaps a religion, or a subculture, or something of that nature. I say former nationality for reasons already stated; however if groups wish to continue to applaud the former stated values, symbolism, songs, and so forth of their nation, that is generally a positive thing.

In the modern period there are many people with few social contacts in the "real" world beyond their workplace, and there's no guarantee the social connections they have made will persist because there is no guarantee that all of their coworkers, friends, acquaintances, or family members are still alive; as such it makes some sense, in a world without borders and with fairly high levels of trade and migration, for people to make it known they were once part of a larger and often international social web when information technology was common.

As such these individuals may attempt to conglomerate and craft their own social orders around loosely agreed upon concepts. If this is done, it should be either for pragmatic reasons or for humor (literally, to reduce their psycho-social stress after the collapse of human civilization) rather than the purpose of, say, creating an army and going to war against those who they felt slighted by before the catastrophic times.

Because of the nature of identifying cues such as symbols or flags, it leaves open the possibility that someone may do as privateers did in the days of old, whereby they would fly the flag of whatever nation was dominant in the region, in an effort to sidle up to their vessels and take them by surprise before the other vessel could realize it was a pirate vessel. While this seems fantastic, it is one risk of using such features alone.

Organized settlements should remain as peaceful as possible internally and externally; the best world man can create once the slate is cleared is one which is well organized but contains as much personal liberty as possible; one in which there is as little moralism and infighting as can be, but in which people are at the same time armed and capable of defending themselves individually or as a group. In this manner, groups should recognize that other groups exist, and should seek not to destroy, conquer, or disturb them, but rather work *with* them even if their own views are separate and different.

Thus it should be possible for those within a settled region to recognize one another. Through the division of labor, in time, there will be those who traverse various areas for trading purposes, and they may consider themselves detached from any loyalty if they wish, since their function will be essential to multiple groups. Those from other regions should not be assumed to be hostile upon being identified as foreign, for it is in this practice that wars can begin, or at least vengeful fighting, which can create a feud.

CULT AVOIDANCE

Now we come to a strange topic but one which has not likely been covered in any other post apocalyptic guide- the topic of cults and their likely existence after the ashes.

When the human psyche has become fractured by witnessing much of the world pass away in nuclear fire, the spread of fanaticism may be a bigger threat than anything other than starvation or epidemic; suicide cults are likely to destroy themselves but homicidal maniacs worshiping the deities of destruction (and quite possibly without understanding the historical basis of the same figures) are very likely to exist. Whenever we regard fictional post apocalyptic accounts, there tends to be some group or several groups which have become a bit insane in the conditions they experience after the crumbling of normal human society. In their frenzied state, they become zealots and either dedicate themselves to spreading by conquest, or isolate themselves and pick off stray travelers for sacrifice, or something like that. While we may regard the idea of, say, a cult of self professed vampires or devil worshiping murderers to be funny, it will not be so amusing when all legal means of suppressing the same have been removed. As I stated, man will regress in mentality where stress is experienced- most humans will quickly obtain the means to survive and will be guided (outside of areas they have substantially organized into society once more) mostly by the simple principles of hunger, fear, sex, and other base emotional tenets.

Areas which are unexplored by whatever social nets come to exist (one organized area or multiple such areas in trade and communication with each other) should be regarded as possible spawning points not just for the occasional pack of feral dogs, or the occasional bear or rabid animal, but also quite possibly for human groups which have views too "far out there" to take part in recognized settlements. We might imagine, a decade after the ashes fall, a semi-walled sort of city state with a few roads and some healthy farming activity, with makeshift towers and everything like a sort of steampunk style medieval fortress, and in the shadows of the same settlement, through a dense pack of forest, an encampment of fanatic blood drinkers who have developed an extraordinarily nihilistic and violent view of the world and which fully intend to rape, enslave, or eat the next person they see that isn't part of their own order.

We would also expect to see the charismatic style of cults propagate themselves, probably more so than the overtly butcherous kind- these charismatics will develop a thousand bizarre social philosophies and rant to anyone who will listen about how to restore the world by adopting some moral or philosophical system. Lest people forget, these same individuals already exist and commonly stand on street corners with signs (often the stereotypical "the end is near" placard.) If they have not attacked anyone they should probably just be left alone, regardless of how annoying they may be, for they too have every right to speak their mind if they are harming nobody.

The re-establishment of organized religion will necessarily take place and will have the same advantages and risks as it has now before any cataclysm has hit. People will benefit from membership insofar as it increases their psychological will to persist, and it may have a positive effect on social order as well, organizing people effectively.

However the risk lies in that people may again become fanatic, or the clergy (however it happens to exist) will misuse their pulpits and stages, or that these religious groups will be co-opted by the unscrupulous and used to support corruption of some kind or another. We see this in the present era; a great deal of (wrongful) support for every so-called patriotic law or war comes from some segment of the clergy, explaining to the untrained laypeople that somehow it was meant to be because of the commands of some distant deity.

Thus there are risks even with what is generally understood to be rather gentle, tolerant religion; this is compounded by the fact that, in the absence of legalism, theocracy may once again try to take root; any attempt by the clergy of any religious order to insinuate itself into the social and legal web of a settled people should be rebuffed, and the clergy chastised for making such an attempt. Lest they declare themselves to be holier than others, those familiar with various tenets of whatever religion they claim should debate them at every possible opportunity should they try and use their spirituality for ill.

NOTES

In conclusion to this work it makes sense to lay out a series of short notes in no particular order; basically tips to allow the survivor a higher chance of continuing to be part of that same classification, rather than to supply a hefty and largely unnecessary end to this work. Here, thus, are a few notations which might be of help.

-Make sure to let some of your crops go to seed without harvesting them, to provide seeds for the subsequent year; this common sense statement may seem like common knowledge to some but some survivors have likely never actually maintained a garden.

-The process of canning using glass bottles is not particularly difficult and should be studied if possible- entire crates of glass jars are available for this, with self-sealing tops. Do not consume anything from a can which has begun to bulge (indicating infection by botulism, which is usually fatal) or which has begun to rust through. Pickling produces toxic gas and should be done in a well ventilated area.

-Coffee will no longer be largely available outside of tropical regions, and will likely command a high price when it first does come back into the markets of the world. Rose hips can be made into a mildly caffeinated tea which also supplies vitamins and is regarded as rather tasty.

-Clothes will begin to degrade over time, and leather may not be widely available either, nor will cotton to any great extent; thankfully this is offset by the massive surplus of clothing which will exist for a time. Humans over a century ago developed semi-mechanized systems for spinning wool and cotton, so the process is not as hard as it may at first seem.

-Because the chief source of warmth for some will be a fireplace and wood, chimney maintenance will be important. There are currently devices on the market which consist of coils of aluminum on a weight which is dropped down the chimney and drawn back up to grind off the creosote which can build up and cause chimney fires or generally prevent the fireplace from emitting as much warmth as it should. Chimney sweeping logs are also available but should not be seen as a permanent solution to the problem.

-It is possible to make charcoal using a steel oil drum which has had holes punched in the bottom to draw air up into a fire rather than down into it in the absence of such holes. The drum is raised a few inches on a semi-circle of dirt and a small hollow left directly under the holes. A fire is started inside and then wooden chunks added to the top and allowed to burn until the smoke thins. It is then mostly closed, with the lid propped open an inch or so, until the smoke becomes pale blue, after which the top lid is sealed and the barrel shaken, then the bottom closed up and the drum allowed to cool for 24 hours or so. The charcoal can be ground up and added to soil as amendment thereof, or can be used for fuel.

-Charcoal is also useful as a toothpaste when ground into a fine powder. Some claim it whitens teeth, but it actually merely removes stains, making it appear to whiten- it is effective at removing plaque, but proper flossing is a necessity in the post apocalyptic world, where a decaying tooth could cause severe problems. Keep your teeth clean, because special diets and dentures may not be available for those who begin to lose their teeth.

-For those who wish to create their own ink, a brew can be made using the outer hulls of black walnuts. Boil the hulls and simmer them until the resulting mix is a dark brown and almost like sludge. I have heard of three other ingredients being variously added; vodka or other clear alcohol, or else vinegar, and sometimes gum arabic.

-If whatever dwelling you are residing in is too chilly, attempt to cover any windows with thick drapes or cloth to reduce draftiness. Furniture- especially book cases- placed against outer walls severely increases the retention of heat in any structure. In Russia, carpets and rugs used to be commonly bolted to outer walls in Soviet times to increase warmth as well as reduce noise pollution in tenements where walls were quite thin; this practice makes sense, and carpeting will be freely available in massive rolls. Simply measure and cut.

-When composting, remember to mix greens and browns; browns consist of cardboard shreds, mulch, wood chips, and bark. Greens consist of most other organic matter (even "brown" grass or leaf clippings.) Adding wood ash to the compost improves it substantially.

-Burning juniper wood can release antimicrobial compounds into the air. White sage has the same property. If a medical setting has been established, these are at least decent substitutes for alcohol and other antiseptic compounds which may not be available.

-The construction of a sort of postmodern Rosetta Stone may be of great help to various cultures which may encounter one another. Allowing the understanding of language to die down will complicate trade and travel in the long term; languages known fluently by members should be transcribed into paragraphs and translated into one another and inscribed on surfaces which can be maintained permanently- carved into stone or otherwise. This would be part of a longer term goal system for recovering humanity as it serves less purpose in the shorter span of time. Such translated stones could be multiplied in number and placed in multiple settled areas.

-After a few decades at most, some maps will be useless because rivers change course with flooding over time and various features will have been destroyed by warfare or erosion and neglect. No map, however well made, should be considered necessarily reliable for all purposes after about twenty years following any major cataclysm.

-Liquor will be important as a medicinal aid and a recreational substance, especially whiskey and gin and other higher-powered alcohols. Guides to distilling are common and the process requires rudimentary knowledge of chemistry and the will to design such a setup.

-Because snow plows will not be widespread and will break down over time or be unable to be fueled, the construction of an Edwardian-era device may be undertaken for the same purpose. This device was horse drawn, and consisted of a massive barrel made of wood which was drawn over a road, to compress the snow down as much as possible, both to delineate where the road was and to make it passable for foot traffic and equestrians, if not for bicycles or modern motor vehicles. Constructing such a thing will require that metalworking be undertaken-this is another use for charcoal.

-Should the war unfold some time from now, many of the problems listed in this work may be ameliorated by the existence of widespread solar and wind power- the former will be crippled by EMP but the means to produce more such panels will exist. The latter will be unaffected by EMP but requires maintenance and may be destroyed by the atomic blasts in some regions.

-Light colored and reflective clothing actually deflects the massive energy of a nuclear explosion rather effectively. There are pictures from Hiroshima of those whose clothing was light colored with dark figures or shapes on it, where the figures and shapes were burned into their flesh, the surrounding skin left intact and largely unharmed.

-The public may or may not get any sort of warning before a nuclear war erupts. There may be no time for a warning or those conducting it may very well choose to simply let the civilians die.

-After any nuclear war, when abandoned buildings are being used for shelter or storage, those in seismically active areas are warned to avoid buildings constructed from brick- which is the least likely to withstand a significant seismic event. Even a single floored wooden structure is more resistant, and some steel frame buildings are built to withstand such events as well. Those living along the Pacific coasts, in the Aegean region, in central Oklahoma, or around the Caribbean are especially at risk.

-There is still debate as to whether a nuclear war will create a fallout winter. Some models presume that even a limited exchange will do so, while others claim that because most nuclear weapons are incapable of sending their ash high enough, such a winter will not occur. In any case, it may be worthwhile to specifically note the presence or absence of such a fallout winter for future reference and to document the event as wholly as possible.

-Abandoned naval vessels may have been washed ashore by tsunamis caused by nuclear explosions. If they are capable of being repaired to any great extent they may provide abundant and extremely adequate shelter.

-It is possible to turn a freight car or any similar box-shaped metallic item into a shelter. Simply install a ventilation system. They can also be used to make fallout shelters, by covering them with earth in a mound or burying them. A few feet of earth is sufficient even near a blast zone to deflect most gamma rays and to provide a rather safe bunker for storing goods and waiting out the contamination.

-The removal of human waste in areas not powered by electricity and which lack steady running water will be a major concern. A simple pit lined with lime can function as a sort of composting toilet, and a simple wooden shack built over it creates an outhouse. This will have to be periodically dredged out, or else moved. Beware of cave-ins below if it is neglected.

-In the case of prolonged cold from fallout winter, or regular winter when fuel is lacking, individuals can sleep together for warmth and merely pile many layers of blankets and clothing on top of themselves to retain heat. So long as they are able to obtain food their own bodies in such a situation can provide adequate (if cramped) warmth.

-For those who wish to learn a great deal about outdoor survival, Ernest Thompson Seton's "Book of Woodcraft" is an especially good choice as a guide thereof, although its lists of edible plants and animal species and so forth are predominantly useful only in North America. It also teaches how to make a simple bow and arrows, which could be invaluable as ammunition for firearms may be impossible to manufacture for some time. It covers everything from constructing a lean-to to building fires, to some songs and guides to types of trees and mushrooms.

-It is possible to grow and raise enough food to feed a person on barely a half acre or so of land. This would include rotated legume and grain crops, various fruit stands, vegetable beds, and probably chickens and perhaps utilitarian crops like cotton (for clothing) or hemp (for rope fibers.)

-The planting of fruit trees, bushes, and vines is a good way to provide enormous amounts of produce with less effort than with plants that require tilling each year or every few years as with most vegetable crops. You will want to obtain a zone map and species able to survive in your zone and learn how to prune the trees or bushes. Pruning, done properly, is important. Grafting is another skill needed for some species to fully produce.

-It is possible to make candle wicks out of mullein plants. The woody stems are rather soft when split into small lengths and can be formed with melted wax into candles should electricity be unavailable.

-Soap can also be made from natural materials; namely fats saponified with lye. The process can be looked up on the internet or in various other books and yields far more soap per batch than a single person would reasonably need. Keep vinegar on hand. Should lye get on your skin immediately neutralize it with a splash of vinegar to prevent a burn.

-Black powder (early gunpowder) can also be made using simply pulverized charcoal, ground up sulfur, and saltpeter. Charcoal is easily made and sulfur easily obtained- as for saltpeter, it is a nitrate compound and was traditionally made by straining urine through straw, collecting the crystals that formed, and purifying them through filtration and reconstitution. Recipes vary although the process is more simple than the creation of modern gunpowder. This process is exceptionally dangerous and should not be merely experimented with. Permits are generally required, as well, to craft and store it.

-Animals thought to be diseased, especially those which may have had rabies, should be destroyed the moment they are killed or as quickly as possible. Do not handle the corpse with bare hands, and burn it to ashes with kerosine or wood.

-Although it sounds morbid, allowing maggots to eat away diseased tissue in a festering wound is preferable to gangrene. Application of clean, lab-raised maggots for this purpose may be the only feasible way to guarantee gangrene treatment that does not involve amputation, for some time after the ashes.

-Modern man is used to wearing socks and shoes almost at all times. While this causes few problems today, this practice should be rethought in a mud-filled ruined world where laundry services are not widely available. Change your socks if they become wet, to prevent issues such as trench foot which could reduce survivability.

-Laundry can be done using an old-style pan method; these are constructed from a wooden frame and metal or wooden bars embedded therein, and the clothes scrubbed over it using lye soap or no soap at all. Drying the laundry is simple- in warm weather hang it on a bush. In cold weather hang it near the fire. It is also possible to simply soak the clothes in a river and beat it with a flat-sided stick.

THE VALUE OF HUMAN LIFE

It suffices here to make one simple final point; the value of human life, and of all life, the absence of which is the sole reason a work like this even needs to be written.

The disparagement of the value of human life has led to all war, to all pain and suffering not caused by nature. It is the poisonous seed from which bigotry, intolerance, xenophobia, and militarism grow like tendrils. It is the innate view of some, towards all or most others, that they are nothing more than robots or automatons, or machinations- little more than the value of their own labor or their own productive capabilities. At the same time, those holding such aberrant views of other human beings often in turn become the most hostile and oppressive, seeing their fellow humans as worth little, and decreasing that perceived worth as well by rendering them into nothing more than thought slaves and work slaves.

Let us all hope that after the ashes this view of humanity is abolished altogether, because otherwise world war three would not be the final war- the final war will come later, be even worse, and finally do such great damage that not one member of our species survives. Whether by the grace of a deity, or our own sentient recognition of self, all humans are due just consideration and liberty.

AN APPEAL TO HUMANITY

To those who have survived, look around you at this moment. Observe the next tree you see. It obeys no laws but those of nature and survival, it has no boss or overlord, it does not ask permission to grow. It does not ask permission to spread.

When the ashes have ended the human race must ask itself one fundamental question; was it happy with the way the world was before, when all was war, paranoia, and corruption, or does it seek something more- something more comforting. Does it wish for a world of ash, or a world of health, with trees and fresh air and clean water? After decades of contamination, will humanity finally realize how valuable freedom and self determination are? How beautiful nature is? Or will he cling once more to the teat of artifice, and beg the same old warlords and butchers to manage affairs so he does not have to make "hard" decisions?

My appeal is this, that mankind should abandon the old ways that led to such a cataclysm in the first place- that natural law be observed, and that the human species embraces itself as too important to bicker, and that its problems may more easily be solved by cooperation and knowledge than by ignorant fighting spurred on by the corrupt and dishonest "leaders" who after all were merely lemmings leading the race off a cliff to its demise.

COPY OF THE BILL OF RIGHTS

AMENDMENT I

Congress shall make no law respecting an establishment of religion, or prohibiting the free exercise thereof; or abridging the freedom of speech, or of the press; or the right of the people peaceably to assemble, and to petition the government for a redress of grievances.

(NOTE: The "press" here refers not just to the news or media but also to publishers, authors, and any and all written or electronic forms of communication available for public consumption. "Speech" also refers to electronic and written speech as well.)

AMENDMENT II

A well regulated militia, being necessary to the security of a free state, the right of the people to keep and bear arms, shall not be infringed.

(NOTE: The US Supreme Court has already cleared up the ambiguity here and declared that the people at large form the militia and are due the right to own firearms and other weapons individually. Disarmament is, and always will be, unconstitutional.)

AMENDMENT III

No soldier shall, in time of peace be quartered in any house, without the consent of the owner, nor in time of war, but in a manner to be prescribed by law.

AMENDMENT IV

The right of the people to be secure in their persons, houses, papers, and effects, against unreasonable searches and seizures, shall not be violated, and no warrants shall issue, but upon probable cause, supported by oath or affirmation, and particularly describing the place to be searched, and the persons or things to be seized.

(NOTE: This includes all private speech, electronic and written communication, and all other variants of transfer of communication presumed to be private.)

AMENDMENT V

No person shall be held to answer for a capital, or otherwise infamous crime, unless on a presentment or indictment of a grand jury, except in cases arising in the land or naval forces, or in the militia, when in actual service in time of war or public danger; nor shall any person be subject for the same offense to be twice put in jeopardy of life or limb; nor shall be compelled in any criminal case to be a witness against himself, nor be deprived of life, liberty, or property, without due process of law; nor shall private property be taken for public use, without just compensation.

AMENDMENT VI

In all criminal prosecutions, the accused shall enjoy the right to a speedy and public trial, by an impartial jury of the state and district wherein the crime shall have been committed, which district shall have been previously ascertained by law, and to be informed of the nature and cause of the accusation; to be confronted with the witnesses against him; to have compulsory process for obtaining witnesses in his favor, and to have the assistance of counsel for his defense.

AMENDMENT VII

In suits at common law, where the value in controversy shall exceed twenty dollars, the right of trial by jury shall be preserved, and no fact tried by a jury, shall be otherwise reexamined in any court of the United States, than according to the rules of the common law.

AMENDMENT VIII

Excessive bail shall not be required, nor excessive fines imposed, nor cruel and unusual punishments inflicted.

AMENDMENT IX

The enumeration in the Constitution, of certain rights, shall not be construed to deny or disparage others retained by the people.

AMENDMENT X

The powers not delegated to the United States by the Constitution, nor prohibited by it to the states, are reserved to the states respectively, or to the people.

Made in the USA
Columbia, SC
29 September 2022